Microsoft© Official Academic Course: Managing and Maintaining a Microsoft Windows Server™ 2003 Environment for an MCSA Certified on Windows© 2000 (70-292)

Lab Manual

D1456419

Dan Holme and Orin Thomas

PUBLISHED BY
Microsoft Press
A Division of Microsoft Corporation
One Microsoft Way
Redmond, Washington 98052-6399

Printed and bound in the United States of America.

1 2 3 4 5 6 7 8 9   QWT   9 8 7 6 5 4

Distributed in Canada by H.B. Fenn and Company Ltd.

A CIP catalogue record for this book is available from the British Library.

Microsoft Press books are available through booksellers and distributors worldwide. For further information about international editions, contact your local Microsoft Corporation office or contact Microsoft Press International directly at fax (425) 936-7329. Visit our Web site at www.microsoft.com/learning/. Send comments to *moac@microsoft.com*.

Microsoft, Active Directory, FrontPage, PowerPoint, Visual Basic, Visual InterDev, Windows, Windows NT, and Windows Server are either registered trademarks or trademarks of Microsoft Corporation in the United States and/or other countries. Other product and company names mentioned herein may be the trademarks of their respective owners.

The example companies, organizations, products, domain names, e-mail addresses, logos, people, places, and events depicted herein are fictitious. No association with any real company, organization, product, domain name, e-mail address, logo, person, place, or event is intended or should be inferred.

This book expresses the author's views and opinions. The information contained in this book is provided without any express, statutory, or implied warranties. Neither the authors, Microsoft Corporation, nor its resellers or distributors will be held liable for any damages caused or alleged to be caused either directly or indirectly by this book.

Acquisitions Editor: Linda Engelman
Project Editor: Denise Bankaitis
Technical Editors: Robert Lyon and Linda Zacker
Copy Editor: Ben Ryan
Production Vendor: Media Services

SubAssy Part No. X10-58493
Body Part No. X10-58485

CONTENTS

LAB 1

INTRODUCTION TO WINDOWS SERVER 2003 FEATURES

Upon completion of this chapter, you will be able to:

- Exercise 1-1: Gathering System Information

- Exercise 1-2: Internet Explorer Enhanced Security Configuration

- Exercise 1-3: Installing Windows Server 2003 Support Tools

- Exercise 1-4: Using Ping and Netdiag to Check Connectivity

- Exercise 1-5: Exploring the Bootcfg Command-line Utility

- Review Questions

- Lab Challenge 1-1: Terminating Processes with Pviewer and Taskkill

SCENARIO

You are a member of the Microsoft Windows Server 2003 pilot program at Contoso, Ltd. Contoso, Ltd. is considering moving to Windows Server 2003 as its primary network operating system. You have just installed two Windows Server 2003 computers in the Contoso, Ltd. development lab. Your manager has asked you to explore some of the features of the product so that you have a better idea of its functionality before the pilot program begins in earnest.

After completing this lab, you will be able to:

- Gather system information about Windows Server 2003.
- Explain the functionality of the new Internet Explorer Enhanced Security Configuration.
- Install the Windows Server 2003 Support Tools.
- Use command-line tools to evaluate network functionality.
- Check the boot configuration of the local and remote computers.

Estimated lesson time: 80 minutes

BEFORE YOU BEGIN

To successfully complete this lab, you will need the following:

- Two networked computers with Windows Server 2003 standalone installed.
- Windows Server 2003 CD-ROM.

> **IMPORTANT** This lab is written to be performed on two computers. If each student has only a single computer, students can work as partners and share computers when needed. The first computer will be Computerxx and the second computer will be Computeryy. Computerxx typically has an odd-numbered name, such as Computer01 and Computer03. Computeryy typically has an even-numbered name, such as Computer02 and Computer04. If you are unsure of your computer's name, open a command prompt and issue the **hostname** command.

EXERCISE 1-1: GATHERING SYSTEM INFORMATION

Estimated completion time: 10 minutes

You have just installed the first two Windows Server 2003 computers in the pilot program. Before you start making changes, you wish to create a report about the current system configuration. To do this, you use the System Information utility included with Windows Server 2003.

> **IMPORTANT** If you have two computers, complete the following tasks on Computerxx. If you are working with a partner, you and your lab partner should separately complete the following tasks on your designated computer.

1. Log on to the computer as Administrator. The password is **P@ssw0rd** or one assigned to you by your instructor

2. Click Start, point to All Programs, point to Accessories, point to System Tools, and then click System Information.

    The System Information window opens.

3. Select the System Summary node in the scope pane (the left window pane) of the System Information window. Review the information provided in the details pane (the right window pane), including the operating system name, version, processor type, and total physical memory, as shown in Figure 1-1.

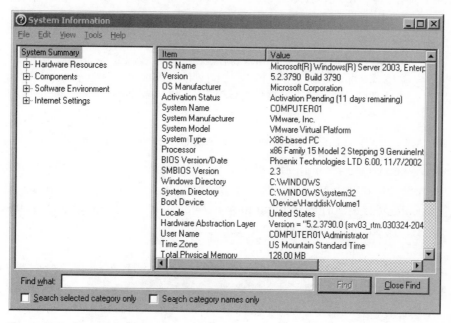

Figure 1-1   System Information

> **QUESTION**   You are interested in storing this information in a text file. How would you export this to a text file named c:\Sysinfo.txt?

4. Expand the Components node and then expand the Storage node. Select the Disks node. Review the information about the disk size, as well as information about any partitions that might exist.

5. Select the Drives node. Notice that this interface now displays not only the individual volumes configured on the disks, but also the size and amount of available free space on each.

6. Close the System Information window.

EXERCISE 1-2: INTERNET EXPLORER ENHANCED SECURITY CONFIGURATION

Estimated completion time: 10 minutes

In reading about Windows Server 2003, you have come across numerous references to the enhanced security features of Microsoft Internet Explorer. These are designed so that server users do not inadvertently introduce malicious code onto the server by viewing Web sites that are untrustworthy. Your manager has asked you to explore the enhanced security features of Internet Explorer and to assess how this will affect using the server to access the Internet.

> **IMPORTANT** If you have two computers, complete the following tasks on Computerxx. If you are working with a partner, you and your lab partner should separately complete the following tasks on your designated computer.

1. While logged on as Administrator, launch Internet Explorer.

    When you first run Internet Explorer on Windows Server 2003 you are presented with a Internet Explorer dialog box showing you that the Enhanced Security Configuration of Microsoft Internet Explorer is currently enabled, as shown in Figure 1-2.

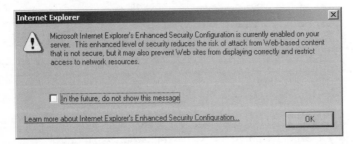

Figure 1-2 Enhanced Security Configuration Information dialog box

2. In this dialog box, select the In The Future Do Not Show This Message check box and then click the Learn More About Internet Explorer's Enhanced Security Configuration link.

    The Internet Explorer Enhanced Security Configuration page is displayed. If the Internet Explorer dialog box appears again, click OK.

> **QUESTION** Which groups of users are able to perform the following tasks:
> a. Turn on/off Internet Explorer Enhanced Security Configuration?
> b. Adjust the security level for a particular zone?
> c. Add sites to the Trusted sites zone?

3. From the Tools menu in Internet Explorer, click Internet Options.

The Internet Options dialog box opens.

4. Select the Security tab as shown in Figure 1-3.

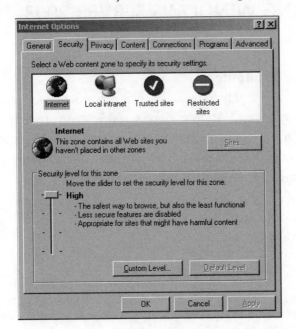

Figure 1-3   The Security tab of the Internet Options dialog box.

5. Click Trusted Sites and then click the Sites button.

The Trusted Sites dialog box opens.

6. In the Add This Web Site To The Zone box, type **http://
    *.microsoft.com** and then click Add to add all sites matching this nam-
    ing format to the zone.

7. Click Close.

> **NOTE**   It is important to realize that the only way to disable Internet
> Explorer Enhanced Security Configuration is to remove it via the Add/
> Remove Windows Components section of the Add Or Remove Programs
> control panel.

> **QUESTION**   Which of the following sites will be included as trusted sites when
> you add http://*.microsoft.com to the zone? (Choose all answers that are
> correct.)
>
> a.   http://www.microsoft.com
> b.   http://microsoft.adatum.com
> c.   http://ftp.microsoft.com
> d.   ftp://ftp.microsoft.com

8. Click OK to close the Internet Options dialog box.

9. Close any open Internet Explorer windows.

EXERCISE 1-3: INSTALLING WINDOWS SERVER 2003 SUPPORT TOOLS

Estimated completion time: 10 minutes

Most of the time, Administrators are able to perform their job functions with the tools that are installed by default with Windows Server 2003. There are times, however, when an Administrator is confronted with a situation where he or she requires more sophisticated tools to assist in diagnosing and resolving computer problems. As a part of your organization's pilot program, your manager has asked you to make an assessment of the Windows Server 2003 Support Tools, an add-on package of tools that is provided with the Windows Server 2003 installation media but that is not installed by default.

> **IMPORTANT**   If you have two computers, complete the following tasks on Computerxx. If you are working with a partner, you and your lab partner should separately complete the following tasks on your designated computer.

1. While logged on to the computer as Administrator, insert the Windows Server 2003 CD. If the Welcome To Microsoft Windows Server 2003 screen appears, click Exit.

2. In the \Support\Tools directory on the CD, double-click the Suptools.msi file.

   The Windows Support Tools Setup Wizard opens.

3. In the Windows Support Tools Setup Wizard, click Next.

4. On the End User License Agreement page, select the I Agree option to accept the license agreement, and then click Next.

5. On the User Information page, enter your name and organization (or leave them as the default) and then click Next.

6. On the Destination Directory page, verify the install path and the available disk space and then click Install Now.

   The installation of the Windows Support Tools begins.

7. When the installation completes, click Finish to exit the wizard.

8. On the Start menu, select All Programs, select Windows Support Tools, and then click Support Tools Help.

The Help And Support Center opens, showing a list of support tools.

QUESTION   Which of the support tools would you use to perform the following functions:

a. Administer BITS

b. Move Active Directory objects to different domains in the same forest

c. View active processes via a GUI

9. Close all open windows.

EXERCISE 1-4: USING PING AND NETDIAG TO CHECK CONNECTIVITY

Estimated completion time: 10 minutes

The Windows Server 2003 pilot program at your company has been provided with several routers and switches that have been kept in storage for a significant amount of time. Your manager has asked you to check whether this equipment is functional and whether the Windows Server 2003 computers connected to it as part of the pilot program are able to communicate with one another. To check that communication is possible via this old networking equipment, you will use utilities included in the Windows Server 2003 default installation as well as in the Windows Server 2003 Support Tools installed in the previous exercise.

IMPORTANT   If you have two computers, complete the following tasks on Computerxx. If you are working with a partner, you and your lab partner should separately complete the following tasks on your designated computer.

1. Open a Command Prompt window. (You can open a command prompt in several ways: type **cmd** in the Run dialog box or click Start, select All Programs, select Accessories, and then select Command Prompt.)

2. At the command prompt type the **ipconfig** command and press ENTER. Note the IP address of the computer.

3. If you have a second computer, repeat the previous step and obtain the IP address of the second computer. If you working with a partner, exchange the computer's IP address information with your partner.

4. Once you have this information, at the command prompt type **ping localhost**, press ENTER, and note the response.

5. At the command prompt type **ping** second-computer-ipaddress (where *second-computer-ipaddress* is the address of the second computer), press ENTER, and note the response.

   The response should be something like:

   ```
   Reply from second-computer-ipaddress: bytes=32 time=1ms TTL=128
   Reply from second-computer-ipaddress: bytes=32 time<1ms TTL=128
   Reply from second-computer-ipaddress: bytes=32 time<1ms TTL=128
   Reply from second-computer-ipaddress: bytes=32 time<1ms TTL=128
   ```

   This indicates that your computer is receiving a response over the network from the second computer.

6. At the command prompt, type **netdiag | more**, press ENTER, and note the response.

   > **NOTE** The "|" character is known as a pipe. Piping the output of a command to another command means that the second command will use the output of the first command as its input.

7. Press the spacebar multiple times to see the output network diagnostic information from the Netdiag command.

   > **QUESTION** Which of the following tests does the Netdiag utility perform? (Choose all answers that are correct.)
   > a. Default gateway test
   > b. Domain membership test
   > c. IP loopback ping test
   > d. DNS zone delegation test

EXERCISE 1-5: EXPLORING THE BOOTCFG COMMAND-LINE UTILITY

Estimated completion time: 10 minutes

The computers that you are using to host Windows Server 2003 in the pilot program are configured with multiple disk drives. This allows you to install Windows Server 2003 on particular drives in specific configurations. At boot time you can select which installation of Windows Server 2003 will run by selecting it from the boot menu. Your manager has asked you to generate a list of each computer in the pilot program's boot configuration. You can do this with the Bootcfg utility.

IMPORTANT If you have two computers, complete the following tasks on Computerxx. If you are working with a partner, you and your lab partner should separately complete the following tasks on your designated computer.

1. In a Command Prompt window, type **bootcfg /?** and then press ENTER. Review the top-level switches associated with the Bootcfg command and their purposes.

2. Type **bootcfg /copy /?** and then press ENTER to view the options associated with the /copy switch.

3. Type **bootcfg /delete /?** and then press ENTER to view the options associated with the /delete switch.

4. Type **bootcfg /query /?** and then press ENTER to view the options associated with the /query switch.

5. Close the Command Prompt window.

QUESTION Under what conditions would you be unable to view the boot configuration of a remote system?

REVIEW QUESTIONS

Estimated completion time: 15 minutes

1. In your own words, describe what you learned during this lab.

2. In what sort of situations should you install the Windows Server 2003 Support Tools?

3. How can you turn off Internet Explorer Enhanced Security Configuration?

4. Which TCP/IP protocol does the Ping utility use to verify connectivity between hosts?

5. Which switch would you use on the Bootfcfg utility to make a backup of current Boot.ini entries?

LAB CHALLENGE 1-1: TERMINATING PROCESSES WITH PVIEWER AND TASKKILL

Estimated completion time: 15 minutes

Run the Calculator utility on the your computer and use the Pviewer utility and Taskkill utilities to stop this application. Describe to your lab instructor the steps that you took to complete this task.

The Pviewer utility, installed as a part of the Windows Server 2003 Support Tools, and the Taskkill utility, included with Windows Server 2003, can be used to terminate processes on local and remote systems. To use Taskkill you need to first run the Tasklist command to identify the task image name or process ID which you will need to pass to the Taskkill command to kill the process. Both of these utilities can be used to terminate processes that cannot be shut down in a more conventional manner.

LAB 2
ACTIVE DIRECTORY INSTALLATION

Upon completion of this chapter, you will be able to:

- Exercise 2-1: Preparing the Server DNS Settings

- Exercise 2-2: Installing Active Directory Using the Active Directory Installation Wizard

- Exercise 2-3: Preparing to Install Active Directory Using Backup Media

- Exercise 2-4: Installing Active Directory Using Backup Media

- Exercise 2-5: Demoting a Domain Controller and Creating a Child Domain

- Exercise 2-6: Configuring a Global Catalog Server

- Review Questions

- Lab Challenge 2-1: Raising the Functional Level of the Forest to Windows Server 2003

SCENARIO

You are the systems administrator for Contoso, Ltd., a large multinational company. Contoso, Ltd. has decided that it wants to implement an entirely new Microsoft Windows Server 2003 infrastructure rather than upgrade its existing servers. You have been asked to run a pilot program where you will upgrade two standalone Windows Server 2003 computers to domain controllers. The first upgrade will be a standard promotion to a domain controller. The second upgrade will be more complex and will use backup media to assist in the domain controller promotion. Next, you will demote the second server and create a child domain controller and configure it as a global catalog server. Finally, you will raise the domain and forest functional levels in preparation for the planned forest environment at Contoso, Ltd.

After completing this lab, you will be able to:

- Upgrade a standalone Windows Server 2003 computer to a domain controller using the Active Directory Installation Wizard.

- Upgrade a standalone Windows Server 2003 computer to a domain controller using a backup of system state data from another domain controller.

- Demote a Windows Server 2003 domain controller to a member server.

- Create a new child domain in an existing Windows Server 2003 domain.

- Convert a Windows Server 2003 computer to a global catalog server.

- Raise the domain and forest functional levels.

Estimated lesson time: 135 minutes

BEFORE YOU BEGIN

To successfully complete this lab, you will need the following:

- Two networked computers with Windows Server 2003 standalone installed.

- Windows Server 2003 CD

> **NOTE** This lab is written to be performed on two computers. If each student has only a single computer, students can work as partners and share computers when needed. The first computer will be Computerxx and the second computer will be Computeryy. Computerxx typically has an odd-numbered name, such as Computer01 and Computer03. Computeryy typically has an even-numbered name, such as Computer02 and Computer04. If you are unsure of your computer's name, open a command prompt and issue the **hostname** command.

EXERCISE 2-1: PREPARING THE SERVER DNS SETTINGS

Estimated completion time: 15 minutes

Active Directory directory service is highly dependent on the Domain Name System (DNS). DNS servers help maintain a consistent namespace for the hosts in a domain. When setting up a new domain, you also configure a DNS server to host the name information for that domain. The Active Directory installation process automatically installs the DNS service on any domain controller that does not have a DNS server already configured. To simulate this for your pilot program, you will change the TCP/IP settings of the Windows Server 2003 computer that you wish to promote to domain controller so that it looks toward itself to resolve DNS requests.

IMPORTANT *Complete the following tasks on Computerxx.*

1. On Computerxx, log on as Administrator. The password is **P@ssw0rd** or one assigned to you by your lab proctor.

2. Open a Command Prompt window, type **ipconfig**, and press Enter. Note the IP address of the computer.

3. Click Start, point to Control Panel, point to Network Connections, right-click Local Area Connection, and then select Properties.

   The Local Area Connection Properties dialog box opens.

4. Select the Internet Protocol (TCP/IP) option and then click Properties.

   The Internet Protocol (TCP/IP) Properties dialog box opens.

5. In the Preferred DNS Server box, type the IP address that you ascertained in Step 2. (The IP address should be the same as the address in the IP Address box.) Figure 2-1 shows the settings for Computer03.

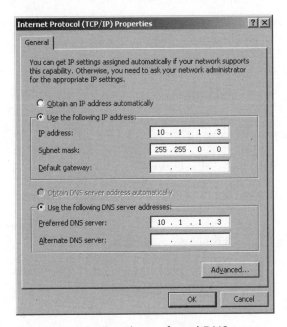

Figure 2-1   Setting the preferred DNS server

6. Click OK to accept your changes.

IMPORTANT *Complete the following tasks on Computeryy*

7. Repeat Step 1, Step 3, Step 4, Step 5, Step 6, and Step 7 on Computeryy. Be sure to use the IP address of Computerxx, not Computeryy, for Computeryy's Preferred DNS Server setting.

QUESTION What advanced options are available on the Advanced tab of the Local Area Connection Properties dialog box? What do they do?

8. Close all open windows on both computers.

EXERCISE 2-2: INSTALLING ACTIVE DIRECTORY USING THE ACTIVE DIRECTORY INSTALLATION WIZARD

Estimated completion time: 20 minutes

The first part of the Windows Server 2003 pilot program at Contoso, Ltd., involves installing Active Directory on the first domain controller in the forest. The Active Directory Installation Wizard provides the most common way to install Active Directory on a Windows Server 2003 computer. Issuing the Dcpromo command starts the Active Directory Installation Wizard.

To install Active Directory on a Windows Server 2003 standalone system and create a new domain in a new forest, complete the following steps:

IMPORTANT Complete the following tasks on Computerxx.

1. On Computerxx, click Start and then click Run.

   The Run dialog box appears.

2. In the Open box, type **dcpromo.exe** and then click OK.

   The Active Directory Installation Wizard launches.

3. On the Welcome To The Active Directory Installation Wizard page, click Next.

4. On the Operating System Compatibility page, click Next.

5. On the Domain Controller Type page, select Domain Controller For A New Domain, as shown in Figure 2-2. Click Next.

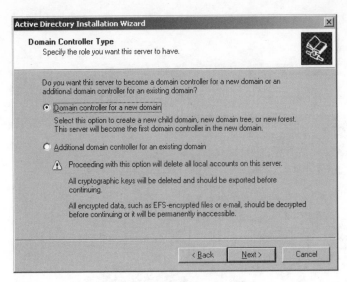

Figure 2-2   Selecting domain controller type

6. On the Create New Domain page, ensure that the Domain In A New Forest option is selected and then click Next.

7. On the New Domain Name page, type the name of your domain in the Full DNS Name For New Domain text box. Your domain is named **contoso***xx***.com** (where *xx* is the number of your computer). Click Next.

8. On the NetBIOS Domain Name page, the Active Directory Installation Wizard will suggest a NetBIOS name (CONTOSO*xx*). Accept the default name provided by clicking Next.

> **QUESTION**   What is the difference between a NetBIOS name and a Full DNS name?

9. On the Database And Log Folders page, accept the defaults by clicking Next.

10. On the Shared System Volume page, leave the default location of the Sysvol folder in the Folder Location box. The Sysvol folder must reside on a partition or volume formatted with the NTFS file system. Click Next.

11. On the DNS Registration Diagnostics page, select the Install And Configure The DNS Server On This Computer option and then click Next.

12. On the Permissions page, read through the available options as shown in Figure 2-3. It is a best practice to accept the default option of Permissions Compatible Only With Windows 2000 Or Windows

Server 2003 Operating Systems. Leave the default option selected and then click Next.

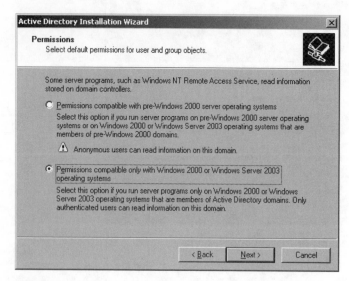

Figure 2-3   The Permissions page of the Active Directory Installation Wizard

13. On the Directory Services Restore Mode Administrator Password page, type the password **P@ssw0rd** in the Restore Mode Password box. It is important to remember that the Directory Services Restore Mode Administrator Password is not necessarily the same as the Administrator password. Many administrators have failed to enter Directory Services Restore Mode because they enter the Administrator password rather than the separate Directory Services Restore Mode Administrator Password. Confirm the password in the Confirm Password box. Click Next.

14. The Summary page displays the options that you have selected through the wizard, as shown in Figure 2-4. Review the contents of this page for accuracy and then click Next.

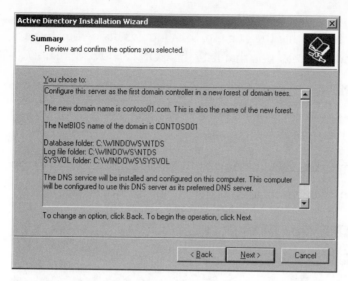

Figure 2-4   Summary page

The wizard takes a few minutes to configure Active Directory components. You might be prompted to insert your Windows Server 2003 CD-ROM.

15. When the Completing The Active Directory Installation Wizard page appears, click Finish and then click Restart Now.

EXERCISE 2-3: PREPARING TO INSTALL ACTIVE DIRECTORY USING BACKUP MEDIA

Estimated completion time: 20 minutes

The second part of the Contoso, Ltd., pilot program will explore a feature new to Windows Server 2003: being able to install Active Directory on a computer using the system state data of an existing domain controller. To be able to perform these actions you need to prepare this system state data from the first Contoso, Ltd. domain controller. In the real world you would then transfer this data via courier to the site where the new domain controller is to be installed. You would also join the second Windows Server 2003 computer to the domain.

To prepare the system state data for use on the second Windows Server 2003 computer perform the following steps:

IMPORTANT   *Complete the following tasks on Computerxx.*

1. On the newly promoted Windows Server 2003 computer, log on as Administrator. Notice that the Log On To Windows dialog box has a Log On To drop-down list box that lists the CONTOSO*xx* domain.

2. Run the Backup utility. Click Start, point to All Programs, Accessories, System Tools, and then click Backup.

   The Backup Or Restore Wizard opens.

3. On the welcome page, click the Advanced Mode link.

   The Backup utility opens in advanced mode (as shown in Figure 2-5).

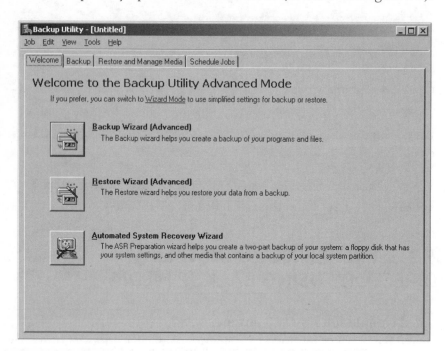

Figure 2-5   The Backup utility running in advanced mode

4. On the Welcome tab, click the Backup Wizard (Advanced) button.

   The Backup Wizard opens.

5. On the welcome page, click Next.

6. On the What To Back Up page, select the Only Back Up The System State Data option. Click Next.

7. On the Backup Type, Destination, And Name page, in the Choose A Place To Save Your Backup drop-down list box, select Let Me Choose A Location Not Listed Here and then click the Browse button.

   A Save As dialog box opens.

8. In the File Name text box, type **c:\backup.bkf** and then click Save.

9. On the Backup Type, Destination, And Name page, click Next.

10. On the Completing The Backup Wizard page, click Finish.

    A Backup Progress dialog box appears indicating the progress of the backup.

    IMPORTANT   *Complete the following tasks on Computeryy.*

    While the backup is occurring on Computerxx, your next steps are to add Computeryy to the domain running on Computerxx.

11. On Computeryy, log on as Administrator.

12. Open the System Properties dialog box. (There are several ways to open the System Properties dialog box: click Start, point to Control Panel, and select System; or click Start, right-click My Computer, and select Properties).

13. On the Computer Name tab, click the Change button.

    The Computer Name Changes dialog box opens.

14. Select the Domain option and type the domain name you specified in Exercise 2-2, which has the form **contoso**xx as shown in Figure 2-6. Click OK.

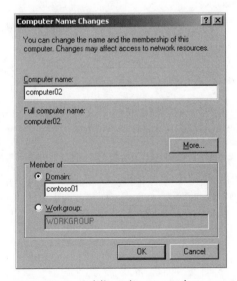

Figure 2-6   Adding the second computer to the domain

A dialog box appears asking for credentials to join the domain. Enter the **Administrator** name and password (**P@ssw0rd**) from the domain controller (Computerxx) and click OK.

15. If the second computer can successfully connect to the domain controller, a welcome message is displayed. Click OK to dismiss the message box.

16. You are informed that you must restart the computer for the changes to take effect. Click OK to dismiss this message box.

17. Click OK to close the System Properties dialog box.

18. The System Settings Change message box informs you that you need to restart the computer. Click Yes to restart the computer now.

IMPORTANT *Complete the following tasks on Computerxx.*

19. On Computerxx, when the backup finishes, close the Backup Progress dialog box and the Backup utility.

20. Create a temporary folder on the C drive named Backup. Move the file C:\Backup.bkf to this folder. You do this so that you can transfer the backup file to Computeryy, though in a real business situation you would copy this backup file to a CD-ROM and courier it to the remote site where you were installing the new domain controller.

21. Open the Properties dialog box for the C:\Backup folder, select the Sharing tab, and then select the Share This Folder option. Then click OK to share the folder on the network.

IMPORTANT *Complete the following tasks on Computeryy.*

22. On Computeryy, open the Log On To Windows dialog box.

23. If the Log On To drop-down list is not visible on the Log On To Windows dialog box, click Options to show additional logon options.

24. Log on as the Administrator of the contosoxx domain. Be certain to select CONTOSOxx in the Log On To drop-down list, as shown in Figure 2-7, and not the local computer.

Figure 2-7   Ensure that you log on to the contoso*xx* domain by specifying the domain in the Log On To drop-down list

25. If the Manage Your Server window appears, select the Don't Display This Page At Logon check box and close the window.

26. Open Windows Explorer, click the Tools menu, and then click Map Network Drive. In the Map Network Drive dialog box, select a drive letter and then type **\\computer*xx*\backup** (the location of the shared backup folder you created on Computer*xx*) in the Folder text box. Clear the Reconnect At Logon check box and then click Finish.

A window showing the contents of the Backup share appears.

27. Open the Backup utility as described in Step 2 of this exercise. This time, when the Backup Or Restore Wizard appears, click Next, staying in wizard mode.

28. On the Backup Or Restore page, select the Restore Files And Settings option and then click Next.

29. On the What To Restore page, click Browse and then browse to the backup file in the mapped network drive.

30. Expand the Items To Restore folder tree until System State is shown. Put a check next to System State as shown in Figure 2-8 and then click Next.

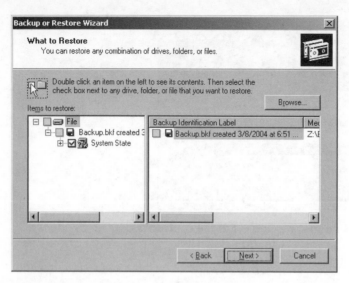

Figure 2-8   Preparing to restore the system state data of the domain controller

31. On the Completing The Backup Or Restore Wizard page, click Advanced to display the Where To Restore page. You must use Advanced because you need to modify the default restore options. If you do not do this you will restore the system state of the domain controller over that of the member server, when you actually need to retrieve the backup of the Active Directory database.

32. In the Restore Files To drop-down list box, select Alternate Location. In the Alternate Location box type **c:\adrestore** as shown in Figure 2-9. Click Next.

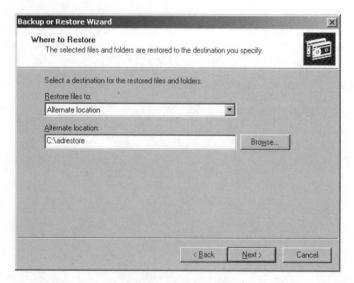

Figure 2-9   Restoring the backed up system state data to an alternate location

33. On the How To Restore page select the Leave Existing Files option and then click Next.

34. On the Advanced Restore Options page, leave the default settings and then click Next.

35. On the summary page, click Finish.

    A Restore Progress dialog box appears.

36. The Restore Progress indicates when the restore process is complete. Close this dialog box and close all open windows on both computers.

EXERCISE 2-4: INSTALLING ACTIVE DIRECTORY USING BACKUP MEDIA

Estimated completion time: 20 minutes

As part of the pilot program, your manager has asked you to test the functionality new to Windows Server 2003: installing Active Directory using either a network share or backup media. The reason for this is because remote offices in Contoso, Ltd.'s organization have very slow wide area network (WAN) links. When a domain controller is installed in a domain and it is not the first domain controller, a copy of the Active Directory database must be replicated to it. If the Active Directory database is large and the WAN link is slow, this replication can take a long time. Sometimes this replication can take so long that it might be quicker to courier out backup tapes with the requisite files.

To install Active Directory using backup media, complete the following steps:

> **IMPORTANT**   *Complete the following tasks on Computeryy.*

1. Open the Run dialog box and issue the **dcpromo /adv** command. When the Active Directory Installation Wizard appears, click Next.

2. On the Operating System Compatibility page, click Next.

3. On the Domain Controller Type page, select the Additional Domain Controller For An Existing Domain option and then click Next.

4. On the Copying Domain Information page shown in Figure 2-10, select From These Restored Backup Files and then type the path to where the backup files have been restored, **c:\adrestore**. Click Next.

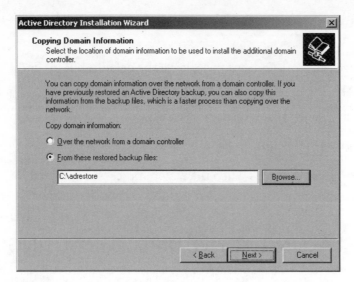

Figure 2-10   Selecting the backed up domain information for restoration

5. On the Global Catalog page, you are asked if you want to configure this domain controller as a global catalog server. Select No and then click Next.

6. On the Network Credentials page, specify the Administrator name and password in the User Name text box and the Password text box, respectively. The Domain text box should be set to contoso*xx*.com. Click Next.

7. On the Database and Log Folders pages, use the default locations for the Database folder and the Log folder as they appear in the Database Folder text box and the Log Folder text box, respectively. Click Next.

8. On the Shared System Volume page, use the default locations for the shared system volume folder which appear in the Folder Location text box. Click Next.

9. On the Directory Services Restore Mode Administrator Password page, type the password **P@ssw0rd** in the Restore Mode Password text box. Confirm the password in the Confirm Password text box. Click Next.

10. On the Summary page, review your selections and then click Next to proceed with the installation of Active Directory based on the backup files of another domain controller.

11. When the Completing The Active Directory Installation Wizard page appears, click Finish and then click Restart Now.

12. Once the computer has restarted, it will be a replica domain controller in the contoso*xx*.com domain. The new domain controller will

replicate with the original, adding any changes to the database that have occurred since creation of the backup that you used to install Active Directory on this second domain controller.

EXERCISE 2-5: DEMOTING A DOMAIN CONTROLLER AND CREATING A CHILD DOMAIN

Estimated Completion Time: 20 minutes

Contoso, Ltd. will eventually implement a Windows Server 2003 forest containing several child domains. To simulate this in the lab, you will create a child domain of the contoso*xx*.com domain. As you currently have only two computer systems with which to simulate the Contoso, Ltd. network, you will need to demote one of them back to member server status before promoting it to be a domain controller in a new domain.

To configure an existing Windows Server 2003 domain controller as a domain controller in a new domain, follow these steps:

IMPORTANT   *Complete the following tasks on Computeryy.*

1. On Computer*yy*, log on as Administrator of the contoso*xx* domain.

2. Click Start and then click Run.

   The Run dialog box appears.

3. In the Open box, type **dcpromo.exe** and then click OK.

4. The Active Directory Installation Wizard launches. You will notice that the dialog box tells you that this computer is already a domain controller and that you can use the wizard to remove Active Directory from this computer. Click Next.

5. On the Remove Active Directory page, shown in Figure 2-11, ensure that you do not select the This Server Is The Last Domain Controller In The Domain option. Click Next

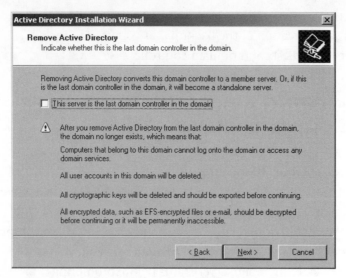

Figure 2-11   The Remove Active Directory page

6. On the Administrator Password page, you are asked to specify a password for the local Administrator account. Enter the following password **P@ssw0rd** twice. Click Next.

7. On the Summary page, review and confirm the options. Click Next.

Active Directory will then be removed from the computer. If you get a message that indicates, "The DSA operation is unable to proceed because of a DNS lookup failure," wait a few minutes for replication to occur and try to remove Active Directory again.

8. When the Completing The Active Directory Installation Wizard page appears, click Finish and then click Restart Now.

9. After Computeryy restarts, log on as Administrator of the contoso*xx* domain using the password **P@ssw0rd**.

10. Click Start and then click Run.

The Run dialog box appears.

11. In the Open box, type **dcpromo.exe** and then click OK.

The Active Directory Installation Wizard opens.

12. On the Welcome To The Active Directory Installation Wizard page, click Next.

13. On the Operating System Compatibility page, click Next.

14. On the Domain Controller Type page, select Domain Controller For A New Domain, as shown earlier in Figure 2-2. Click Next.

15. On the Create New Domain page, select Child Domain In An Existing Domain Tree, as shown in Figure 2-12. Click Next.

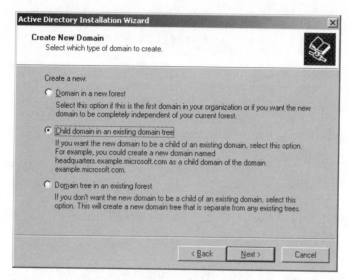

Figure 2-12   Create a new child domain in an existing domain tree.

16. On the Network Credentials page, enter the **Administrator** username and the password **P@ssw0rd**. Ensure that the domain is set to con-toso*xx*.com. Click Next.

17. On the Child Domain Installation page, enter the full DNS name of the parent domain. You can use the Browse button to select **con-toso*xx*.com**. You also will need to enter the child domain name. Enter **contoso***yy* (where *yy* is the number of Computer*yy*). The Child Domain Installation page is shown in Figure 2-13. Click Next.

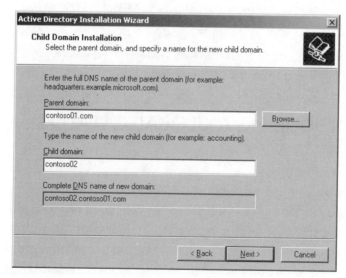

Figure 2-13   Create a new child domain.

18. On the NetBIOS Domain Name page, the Active Directory Installation Wizard will suggest a NetBIOS name (CONTOSOyy). Accept the default name provided by clicking Next.

19. On the Database And Log Folders page, accept the defaults by clicking Next.

20. On the Shared System Volume page, leave the default location of the Sysvol folder in the Folder Location box. Click Next.

21. On the DNS Registration Diagnostics page, you should receive a note that DNS registration support for this domain controller has been verified. Click Next.

> **QUESTION**   Why don't you have to install a new DNS server for the child domain?

22. On the Permissions page, leave the default option selected and then click Next.

23. On the Directory Services Restore Mode Administrator Password page, type the password **P@ssw0rd** in the Restore Mode Password box. Click Next.

24. The Summary page will be displayed. It will be similar to Figure 2-4, but with a different domain name. Note that the summary will also mention that the new domain is a child domain of contosoxx.com. Click Next.

25. The wizard will take a few minutes to configure Active Directory. You might be prompted to insert your Windows Server 2003 CD-ROM.

26. When the Completing The Active Directory Installation Wizard page appears, click Finish and then click Restart Now.

EXERCISE 2-6: CONFIGURING A GLOBAL CATALOG SERVER

Estimated Completion Time: 5 minutes

Although the first domain controller you installed in your pilot program already houses a global catalog server, you want to become familiar with the process of configuring global catalog servers as you intend to eventually place them at all Contoso, Ltd. sites where Microsoft Exchange Server 2003 will also be installed. Global catalog servers speed up queries of information located in other domains within the forest. Because Contoso will eventually move to a forest with many domains, the placement of global catalog servers will be critical to ensuring network responsiveness.

> **IMPORTANT** *Complete the following tasks on Computeryy.*

1. On Computeryy, log on as Administrator of the contosoyy domain.

2. From the Administrative Tools menu, open Active Directory Sites and Services.

3. In the scope pane, expand Sites\Default-First-Site-Name\Servers\Computeryy.

4. Right-click NTDS Settings and click Properties.

   The NTDS Setting Properties dialog box opens.

5. On the General tab, select the Global Catalog check box.

6. Click OK to close the Properties dialog box and then close Active Directory Sites and Services.

REVIEW QUESTIONS

Estimated completion time: 20 minutes

1. In your own words, describe what you learned during this lab.

2. Why, in Exercise 2-2, were you asked to configure a domain in a new forest? Why not configure a domain within an existing forest?

3. In what cases would you select alternate permissions for Step 12 of Exercise 2-2?

4. Why does the normal Administrator account password not always work in Directory Services Restore Mode?

5. Why does a domain controller hosting a DNS server require a static IP address?

6. You are restoring the system state data of a domain controller to a member server. You are doing this in preparation for using that data in the process of promoting the member server to host the Active Directory database. Why is it important, when restoring the system state data of another domain controller on a member server, to specify an alternate location?

LAB CHALLENGE 2-1: RAISING THE FUNCTIONAL LEVEL OF THE FOREST TO WINDOWS SERVER 2003

Estimated Completion Time: 15 minutes

After reading more about Windows Server 2003 in your research for the pilot program, you have determined that you need to raise the functional level of your forest to Windows Server 2003. This will allow you to take full advantage of all of the new features of Windows Server 2003.

IMPORTANT   *Complete the following task on Computerxx.*

- Using the Active Directory Domains and Trusts console, raise the forest functional level to Windows Server 2003.

- At the end of the process, provide a screenshot for your instructor that shows that the forest functional level is set to Windows Server 2003 and cannot be raised further. You can take a screenshot of the entire screen by pressing PRINTSCREEN, or you can take a screenshot of the active window by pressing ALT+PRINTSCREEN. Then, open Microsoft Paint and from the Edit menu select Paste. Save the resulting picture for submission.

LAB 3
EXPLORING GROUP POLICY OBJECTS

Upon completion of this chapter, you will be able to:

- Exercise 3-1: Installing the Group Policy Management Console

- Exercise 3-2: Determine Where to Link GPOs

- Exercise 3-3: Creating and Configuring a New GPO

- Exercise 3-4: Deleting a GPO

- Exercise 3-5: Setting GPO Options and Blocking Inheritance

- Exercise 3-6: Filtering GPO Scope

- Exercise 3-7: Disabling GPO Settings

- Review Questions

- Lab Challenge 3-1: Denying Access to Microsoft Paint

- Lab Challenge 3-2: Denying Access to Registry Editing

SCENARIO

You are a domain administrator for Contoso, Ltd. Contoso, Ltd. has a large multi-domain Active Directory network with contoso.com as its root domain. You are responsible for implementing Group Policy settings at the site, domain, and organizational unit (OU) levels. Contoso, Ltd. recently implemented the contoso.com Active Directory domain. IT management has just signed off on the final OU design and has created a list of approved Group Policy settings.

After completing this lab, you will be able to:

- Install the Group Policy Management Console.

- Determine where to link GPOs.

- Create and edit GPOs.

- Use Gpupdate to refresh Group Policy settings.

- Configure GPO options.

- Modify the scope of a GPO.

- Disable Computer Configuration or User Configuration policies.

Estimated lesson time: 115 minutes

BEFORE YOU BEGIN

To successfully complete this lab, you will need the following:

- A computer with Windows Server 2003 installed and configured as a domain controller. (See Lab Exercises 2-1 and 2-2.)

- The computer should have its own domain, which will either be named contosoxx.com or contosoyy.contosoxx.com.

- The domain functional level must be set to Windows 2000 native or Windows Server 2003. (See Lab Challenge 2-1).

> **NOTE**   This lab is written to be performed on two computers. If each student has only a single computer, students can work as partners and share computers when needed. The first computer will be Computerxx and the second computer will be Computeryy. Computerxx typically has an odd-numbered name, such as Computer01 and Computer03. Computeryy typically has an even-numbered name, such as Computer02 and Computer04. If you are unsure of your computers name, run a command prompt and issue the **hostname** command.

EXERCISE 3-1: INSTALL THE GROUP POLICY MANAGEMENT CONSOLE

Estimated completion time: 5 minutes

You have been reading Microsoft's TechNet articles and have come across many references to the Group Policy Management console (GPMC). This console extends the functionality of the Active Directory Users and Computers console as well as enabling Group Policy modeling which will allow you to view the impact of policies before they are applied to sites, domains, or organizational units. As part of the Contoso, Ltd. pilot program, you wish to install the Group Policy Management console on all domain controllers within the Contosoxx.com forest.

> **IMPORTANT**   If you have two computers, complete the following tasks on Computerxx. If you are working with a partner, you and your lab partner should separately complete the following tasks on your designated computer.

1. Log on as Administrator. The password is **P@ssw0rd** or one assigned to you by your lab proctor. For Computerxx, select the contosoxx domain. For Computeryy, select the contosoyy domain.

2. Using Windows Explorer, open the C:\Lab Manual\Lab03 folder.

3. Double-click Gpmc.msi to start the installation of the Group Policy Management console.

   The Microsoft Group Policy Management Console Setup Wizard opens.

4. On the welcome page, click Next.

5. On the License Agreement page, review the terms, select I Agree, and then click Next.

6. When the installation finishes, click Finish.

EXERCISE 3-2: DETERMINE WHERE TO LINK GPOS

Estimated completion time: 5 minutes

The approved list of Group Policy settings calls for the entire contoso.com domain to have certain standardized configurations for users' desktops. The approved list includes removing the Run command from every user's Start menu and locking the taskbar. These settings should apply to every user in the contoso.com domain.

> **QUESTION**   How and where should you apply these Group Policy settings?
>
> a.   Create a GPO with these settings and link it to the contoso.com domain.
>
> b.   Add these settings to the Default Domain Policy for the contoso.com domain.
>
> c.   Create a GPO with these settings and link it to each of the three first-level OUs for the contoso.com domain.

d. Create a new GPO with these settings and link it to the Users container in the contoso.com domain.

e. Create a GPO with these settings and link it to only one of the first-level OUs for the contoso.com domain.

EXERCISE 3-3: CREATING AND CONFIGURING A NEW GPO

Estimated completion time: 10 minutes

You now need to create a new GPO for the contoso.com domain and configure its settings based on the list approved by management.

> **IMPORTANT** If you have two computers, complete the following tasks on Computerxx. If you are working with a partner, you and your lab partner should separately complete the following tasks on your designated computer.

1. Click Start, point to Administrative Tools, and click Active Directory Users And Computers.

    The Active Directory Users And Computers console opens.

2. Right-click the contoso*xx*.com (or contoso*yy*.contoso*xx*.com) domain icon in the scope pane and select Properties.

    The Properties dialog box for the domain opens.

3. Select the Group Policy tab and then click Open to open the Group Policy Management console.

4. Right-click the contoso*xx*.com (or contoso*yy*.contoso*xx*.com) domain icon in the scope pane and select Create And Link A GPO Here as shown in Figure 3-1.

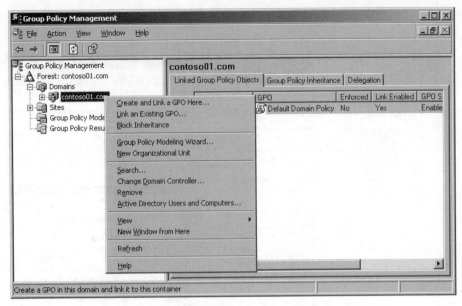

Figure 3-1   Create and link a GPO in the Group Policy Management console.

The New GPO dialog box opens.

5. In the Name box, type **Domain Desktop Settings** and then select OK.

A new GPO named Domain Desktop Settings should appear in the list of GPOs linked to the contosoxx.com (or contosoyy.contosoxx.com) domain.

6. Right-click the Domain Desktop Settings GPO and select Edit.

The Group Policy Object Editor opens.

7. In the scope pane, expand the User Configuration\Administrative Templates\Start Menu And Taskbar node.

The available settings for the Start Menu And Taskbar policy appear in the details pane in Extended view.

8. Select the Remove Run Menu From Start Menu setting.

Explanation text for this setting appears just to the left of the list of settings when displayed in Extended view, as shown in Figure 3-2.

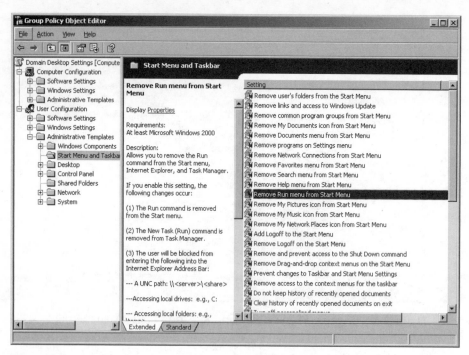

Figure 3-2   The Group Policy Object Editor, with settings for the Start Menu And Taskbar policy in the details pane

9. Select the Standard tab at the bottom of the window to display the Standard view.

10. Double-click the Remove Run Menu From Start Menu setting to display its Properties dialog box.

11. Select the Enabled option and then click OK to turn on this policy setting.

   The State column in the Group Policy Object Editor should now display Enabled instead of Not Configured for this setting.

12. Double-click the Lock The Taskbar setting to display its Properties dialog box.

13. Select the Enabled option and then click OK to turn on this policy setting.

   The State column should now display Enabled instead of Not Configured for this setting.

   QUESTION   What effect does enabling this setting have?

14. Close the Group Policy Object Editor, close the Group Policy Management console, and close the domain Properties dialog box.

15. Open a Command Prompt window, type **gpupdate**, and press ENTER.

   The Gpupdate command refreshes GPOs on the system.

16. To ensure GPOs are updated, log off and log on again.

   QUESTION Does the Run command appear on the Start menu? Can you drag the taskbar from the bottom to the side of the computer screen?

EXERCISE 3-4: DELETING A GPO

Estimated completion time: 5 minutes

To restore the Run menu and allow the taskbar to be moved, you need to unlink or delete the Domain Desktop Settings GPO you created in Exercise 3-3.

   IMPORTANT If you have two computers, complete the following tasks on Computerxx. If you are working with a partner, you and your lab partner should separately complete the following tasks on your designated computer.

1. In Active Directory Users and Computers, right-click the contosoxx.com (or contosoyy.contosoxx.com) domain icon in the scope pane and select Properties.

2. Select the Group Policy tab and then click Open to open the Group Policy Management console.

3. On the Linked Group Policy Objects tab for the contosoxx.com (or contosoyy.contosoxx.com) domain, right click the Domain Desktop Settings GPO link and click Delete.

   A dialog appears informing you that this will delete the link, but not the GPO.

4. Click OK to remove the link.

5. Close the Group Policy Management console, close the domain Properties dialog box, and then close Active Directory Users and Computers.

6. Using Gpupdate, refresh Group Policy on the system, as described in Step 15 of Exercise 3-3.

7. Verify that Run appears on the Start menu and verify that you can move the taskbar. (If this is not the case, log off and log on again to update your policy settings.)

EXERCISE 3-5: SETTING GPO OPTIONS AND BLOCKING INHERITANCE

Estimated completion time: 20 minutes

Your manager instructs you to create a new first-level OU named Human Resources. Under the Human Resources OU, you are told to create two second-level OUs, one named Staff and one named Managers.

You are asked to stop Group Policy settings for the contoso.com domain from affecting users in the Human Resources OU and below. You are also put in charge of creating a new Group Policy named HR Settings for the Human Resources OU that will affect both the Staff and Managers OUs. The Staff and Managers OUs must allow the new policy settings to apply under all circumstances.

> **IMPORTANT**   If you have two computers, complete the following tasks on Computerxx. If you are working with a partner, you and your lab partner should separately complete the following tasks on your designated computer.

1. Open Active Directory Users And Computers.

2. Right-click the contosoxx.com (or contosoyy.contosoxx.com) domain object in the scope pane, point to New, and click Organizational Unit.

   The New Object – Organizational Unit dialog box opens.

3. Type in the name for this new OU, **Human Resources**, and click OK.

4. Right-click the Human Resources OU object in the scope pane, point to New, and click Organizational Unit.

5. Type in the name for this new OU, **Managers**, and click OK.

6. Right-click the Human Resources OU object in the scope pane, point to New, and click Organizational Unit.

7. Type in the name for this new OU, **Staff**, and click OK. Active Directory Users and Computers should look similar to Figure 3-3.

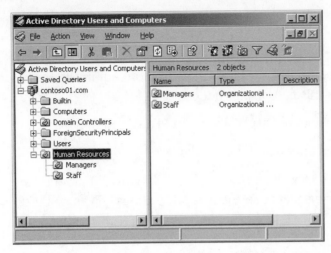

Figure 3-3   OUs added to Active Directory Users and Computers

8. Right-click the Human Resources OU and select Properties.

The Human Resources Properties dialog box opens.

9. Select the Group Policy tab and then click Open to open the Group Policy Management console.

10. In the Group Policy Management console, right-click the Human Resources OU and select Block Inheritance.

A small blue icon appears on the Human Resources OU.

> **QUESTION**   What does this setting accomplish?

11. Right-click again the Human Resources OU and select Create And Link GPO Here.

The New GPO dialog box opens.

12. In the Name box, type **HR Settings** and then click OK.

13. Right-click the HR Settings GPO link and then select Edit.

The Group Policy Object Editor appears.

14. In the scope pane, expand the Computer Configuration\Administrative Templates\Windows Components\Windows Messenger node.

15. Double-click the Do Not Allow Windows Messenger To Be Run setting in the details pane.

The Properties dialog box for the setting opens.

16. Select the Enabled option and click OK.

QUESTION   What does the Do Not Allow Windows Messenger To Be Run setting do?

17. In the scope pane, expand the User Configuration\Administrative Templates\Control Panel\Display node.

18. Double-click the Remove Display In Control Panel setting.

19. Select the Enabled option and then click OK.

20. Close the Group Policy Object Editor. This will return you to the Group Policy Management console. The HR Settings GPO should still be selected.

QUESTION   What does the Remove Display In Control Panel setting do?

QUESTION   How can you force users and computers in the Staff and Mangers OUs to accept the settings configured in the HR Settings GPO, even if Block Inheritance is enabled?

21. Right-click the HR Settings policy and select Enforced.

A dialog box appears asking if you wan to change the Enforced setting.

22. Click OK.

23. Close the Group Policy Management console, close the Human Resources Properties dialog box, and then close Active Directory Users And Computers.

EXERCISE 3-6: FILTERING GPO SCOPE

Estimated completion time: 10 minutes

Both the Staff OU and the Managers OU contain help desk personnel that require the ability to work with display settings and Windows Messenger. Since the Enforced option has been set for the HR Settings GPO link, you must find a way to provide access to both of these features to the help desk users who are contained in the Human Resources\Staff OU. Assume that all help desk personnel are members of the Account Operators domain local security group.

IMPORTANT   If you have two computers, complete the following tasks on Computerxx. If you are working with a partner, you and your lab partner should separately complete the following tasks on your designated computer.

1. Open Active Directory Users And Computers.

2. Right-click the Human Resources OU and select Properties.

    The Human Resources Properties dialog box opens.

3. Select the Group Policy tab and then click Open to open the Group
    Policy Management console.

    The Human Resources OU should be selected.

4. Click the Group Policy Inheritance tab as shown in Figure 3-4.

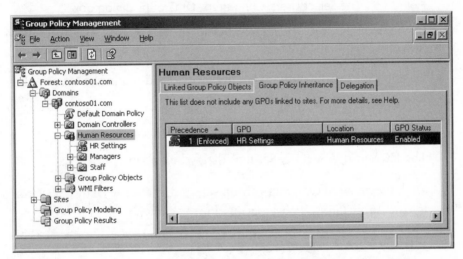

Figure 3-4   The Group Policy Inheritance tab in the Group Policy Management console.

5. Double click the HR Settings policy.

    A warning will be displayed informing you that changes made are glo-
    bal to the GPO.

6. Click OK.

7. In the Security Filtering section, click Add.

    The Select Users, Computers, Or Groups dialog box opens, as shown
    in Figure 3-5.

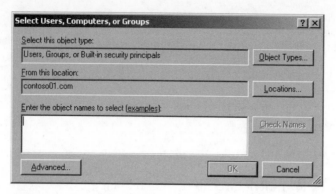

Figure 3-5 The Select Users, Computers, Or Groups dialog box

8. In the Enter The Object Names To Select text box, type **Account Operators** and then click OK.

   An entry for the Account Operators group is added in the Security Filtering list.

9. Click the Delegation tab and then click Advanced.

   The HR Settings Security Settings dialog box opens.

10. With the Account Operators group selected, mark the Deny check box for the Apply Group Policy permission, as shown in Figure 3-6.

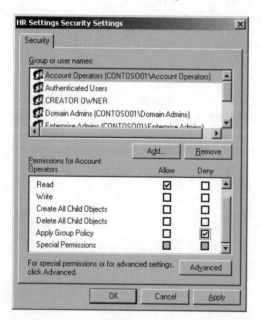

Figure 3-6 Denying a group's Apply Group Policy permission to a GPO link

11. Click OK.

   A Security message box appears warning you that deny permission entries always take precedence over allow entries.

12. Click Yes in the Security message box.

> **QUESTION**   The Authenticated Users special group includes *all* users in a domain. That means that users who are members of the Account Operators group are also Authenticated Users. Why does this step prevent the policies from applying to these users, when the Allow: Apply Group Policy permission is already in effect?

13. Close the Group Policy Management console, close the Human Resources Properties dialog box, and then close Active Directory Users And Computers.

EXERCISE 3-7: DISABLING GPO SETTINGS

Estimated completion time: 10 minutes

For the next two weeks, users in the Human Resources, Staff, and Managers OUs will need to make various changes to their display settings. Management has agreed to this temporary change.

You are now asked to temporarily turn off the restriction on changing display settings, as well as any other User Configuration settings that may exist within the HR Settings GPO.

> **IMPORTANT**   If you have two computers, complete the following tasks on Computerxx. If you are working with a partner, you and your lab partner should separately complete the following tasks on your designated computer.

1. Open Active Directory Users And Computers.

2. Right-click the Human Resources OU and select Properties.

     The Human Resources Properties dialog box opens.

3. Select the Group Policy tab and then click Open to open the Group Policy Management console.

4. In the scope pane, select the HR Settings policy.

     You will be presented with a warning informing you that changes are global to the GPO.

5. Click OK.

6. Click the Details tab.

7. In the GPO Status drop-down list, select User Configuration Settings Disabled.

A message appears asking if you want to change the status of the GPO.

8. Click OK.

The Details tab should be similar to Figure 3-7.

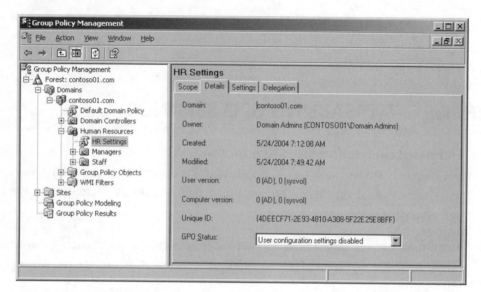

Figure 3-7   Disabling the User configuration settings for the HR Settings GPO

> **QUESTION**   *Do Computer Configuration settings still apply?*

> **QUESTION**   *How can you easily disable the entire GPO?*

9. In the scope pane, right-click the HR Settings GPO and select Link Enabled to remove the checkmark next to Link Enabled.

10. Close the Group Policy Management console, close the Human Resources Properties dialog box, and then close Active Directory Users and Computers.

REVIEW QUESTIONS

Estimated completion time: 15 minutes

1. In your own words, describe what you learned during this lab.

2. How can you exempt various users or groups from a domain-wide policy?

3. How does inheritance of Group Policy apply to child OUs?

4. How can you immediately apply updates with Group Policy settings?

5. How can you block the Enforced option for Group Policy settings that are configured on a parent container?

LAB CHALLENGE 3-1: DENYING ACCESS TO MICROSOFT PAINT

Estimated completion time: 15 minutes

You are a network administrator for the contoso.com domain. You have been asked to configure Group Policy to deny access to the Microsoft Paint utility to everyone in the domain.

Create a new GPO named "Deny MSPaint" using the policy setting located at User Configuration\Administrative Templates\System\Don't Run Specified Windows Applications. To prove you have been successful, refresh Group Policy on your computer and try running the Paint utility.

What message do you receive when you try running Paint by clicking Start, pointing to All Programs, pointing to Accessories, and selecting Paint? What happens when you enter **mspaint** at the command-line?

LAB CHALLENGE 3-2: DENYING ACCESS TO REGISTRY EDITING

Estimated completion time: 15 minutes

You are a network administrator for the contoso.com domain. You have been asked to configure Group Policy to deny access to registry editing tools to everyone except the members of the Domain Admins security group.

Create a new GPO named "Deny Registry Editing" using the policy setting located at User Configuration\Administrative Templates\System\Prevent Access

To The Registry Editing Tools and apply it to everyone except members of the Domain Admins security group, for which you must deny the Apply Group Policy attribute. Use the Gpresult command-line utility to confirm this. For information on using the Gpresult command, type **gpresult /?** at a command prompt.

What does the output of the Gpresult command say about the Deny Registry Editing GPO in the The Following GPOs Were Not Applied Because They Were Filtered Out section?

POST-LAB CLEANUP

Estimated completion time: 5 minutes
Delete the following GPOs created in these Lab Challenges (Reference Lab Exercise 3-4). Do *not* delete the Default Domain Policy GPO.

- Deny MSPaint
- Deny Registry Editing

LAB 4

MANAGING USERS AND GROUPS

Upon completion of this chapter, you will be able to:

- Exercise 4-1: Creating User Objects

- Exercise 4-2: Modifying User Object Properties

- Exercise 4-3: Creating Security and Distribution Groups

- Exercise 4-4: Managing Group Membership

- Exercise 4-5: Changing Group Types and Scopes

- Exercise 4-6: Configuring Account Policies

- Exercise 4-7: Generating and Examining Logon Events

- Review Questions

- Lab Challenge 4-1 : Modifying the Properties of Multiple User Objects

SCENARIO

You are a part of the domain Administration team at Contoso, Ltd. Contoso, Ltd. thas a large single-domain network with contoso.com as the domain root. You are responsible for the management of user and group accounts within the contoso.com domain. Contoso, Ltd. has recently migrated to Microsoft Windows Server 2003 and your team leader has asked you to review user and group account creation methods on the new operating system. Although you expect that many tasks will be familiar, it is important that you are able to use Windows Server 2003 tools for the management of users and groups. As your duties include the management of user and group accounts, your job description lists the following responsibilities:

After completing this lab, you will be able to:

- Creating new user objects for members of staff who have joined the company.

- Making appropriate modifications to existing user objects as required.

- Creating and managing security and distribution groups used in the contoso.com domain.

- Create user and group objects in Windows Server 2003.

- Modify the properties of user objects in Windows Server 2003.

- Create and manage security and distribution groups, including group membership and group scope.

- Modify the properties of multiple user objects at a single time.

- Configure account policies.

- Generate and examine logon events.

Estimated lesson time: 110 minutes

BEFORE YOU BEGIN

To successfully complete this lab, you will need the following:

- A computer with Windows Server 2003 installed and configured as a domain controller. (See Lab Exercises 2-1 and 2-2.)

- The computer should have its own domain, which will either be named contosoxx.com or contosoyy.contosoxx.com.

- The domain functional level must be set to Windows 2000 native or Windows Server 2003. (See Lab Challenge 2-1.)

- Have installed the Group Policy Management console. (See Lab Exercise 3-1.)

> **NOTE**   This lab is written to be performed on two computers. If each student has only a single computer, students can work as partners and share computers when needed. The first computer will be Computerxx and the second computer will be Computeryy. Computerxx typically has an odd-numbered name, such as Computer01 and Computer03. Computeryy typically has an even-numbered name, such as Computer02 and Computer04 . If you are unsure of your computers name, run a command prompt and issue the **hostname** command.

EXERCISE 4-1: CREATING USER OBJECTS

Estimated completion time: 10 minutes

Four new employees have begun work this week at Contoso, Ltd. You have been contacted by the Human Resources department to create user accounts for these users. To create these accounts, you log on to the console of the domain controller for your domain and perform the following steps.

> **IMPORTANT** If you have two computers, complete the following tasks on Computerxx. If you are working with a partner, you and your lab partner should separately complete the following tasks on your designated computer.

1. Log on to the computer as Administrator. The password is P@ssw0rd or one assigned to you by your lab proctor. For Computerxx, select the contosoxx domain. For Computeryy, select the contosoyy domain.

2. Open Active Directory Users and Computers.

3. In the scope pane, right-click the Users container, point to New, and then select User.

   The New Object – User wizard launches.

4. Enter the following information on the first page of the wizard, as shown in Figure 4-1.

Text Box Name	Type
First Name	Dan
Last Name	Holme
User Logon Name	dan.holme
User Logon Name (Pre–Windows 2000)	dholme

5. Click Next.

6. On the second page of the wizard, enter and confirm a strong password for the new user. You should experiment and develop your own strong password. Make a note of this password and then click Next.

> **IMPORTANT** **Strong Passwords** Strong passwords must contain at least three of these four types of characters: uppercase letters, lowercase letters, numerals, and non-alphanumeric characters. They also must be a minimum of seven characters in length and not contain elements of the user's name.

7. Verify the information presented in the summary page of the wizard and then click Finish.

The Dan Holme user object is created and added to the Users container.

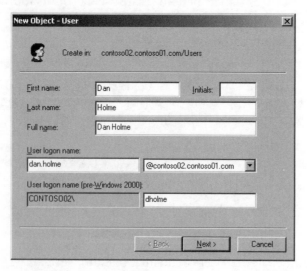

Figure 4-1   Creating a new user in the New Object – User wizard

8. Repeat Steps 3 through 7 to create three more user objects with the following properties:

Property	User1	User2	User3
First Name	Orin	Oksana	Rooslan
Last Name	Thomas	Sitnikova	Lee
User Logon Name	orin.thomas	oksana.sitnikova	rooslan.lee
User Logon Name (Pre–Windows 2000)	othomas	ositnikova	rlee

QUESTION   Which of the following passwords meet the strong password requirements of Windows Server 2003?

    a.   cryptographic

    b.   Pa5#

    c. $1$2$3$4

    d.   AbCd1@3$

QUESTION   What are the four password check-box options?

EXERCISE 4-2: MODIFYING USER OBJECT PROPERTIES

Estimated completion time: 10 minutes

You have received more information about two new employees of your organization, Rooslan Lee and Oksana Sitnikova. Your manager has asked you to add the following properties to these accounts, as listed in the table below:

Property	Oksana Sitnikova	Rooslan Lee
Office	247A	321B
Address	123 Short St	123 Short St
City	Melbourne	Melbourne
State/Province	Victoria	Victoria
Zip/Postal Code	3001	3001
Country/region	Australia	Australia
Title	Marketing Manager	Senior Engineer
Department	Sales and Marketing	Computer Support

IMPORTANT If you have two computers, complete the following tasks on Computerxx. If you are working with a partner, you and your lab partner should separately complete the following tasks on your designated computer.

1. In Active Directory Users and Computers, select the Users container.

2. Open the Properties dialog box for the Oksana Sitnikova user object created in the previous exercise.

3. Select the General tab and enter **247A** in the Office text box.

4. Select the Address tab, and enter the values for the Address, City, State/Province, Zip/Postal Code, and Country/region properties, as given in the preceding table. The Address tab is shown in Figure 4-2.

5. Select the Organization tab and enter the values for the Title and Department properties.

6. Examine the many properties associated with this user object, but do not change any other properties yet.

QUESTION On which tab are the following properties located: Mobile, Fax, Allow Dial-in Access, Idle Session Limit, and Manager?

7. Click OK to close the Properties dialog box.

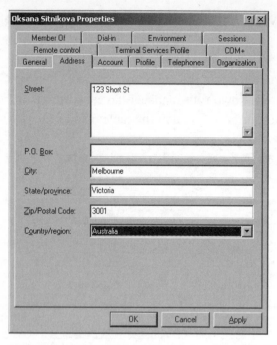

Figure 4-2   The Address tab of a user object's Properties dialog box

8. Repeat Steps 2 through 6 for the Rooslan Lee object, entering the appropriate values from the preceding table.

EXERCISE 4-3: CREATING SECURITY AND DISTRIBUTION GROUPS

Estimated completion time: 10 minutes

Recent restructuring in your organization has lead to the creation of two new departments: Marketing and Sales. Your organization has also just opened a branch office in New York. The Marketing department will contain a subdivision, International Marketing. The Sales department will have personnel that will handle two types of sales, Domestic and International. Your manager has asked you to create new groups for all of these categories by completing the following steps.

> **IMPORTANT**   If you have two computers, complete the following tasks on Computerxx. If you are working with a partner, you and your lab partner should separately complete the following tasks on your designated computer.

1. In Active Directory Users and Computers, right-click the Users container, point to New, and then select Group.

    The New Object – Group dialog box opens.

2. In the New Object – Group dialog box, type **Marketing** in the Group Name text box. Ensure that the Global option is selected under Group Scope and that the Security option is selected under Group Type. Click OK.

   The Marketing global security group is created and added to the Users container.

   > **QUESTION**   When you create a new group, there are two options for group type and three options for group scope. What are these options?

3. Create an additional global security group in the Users container named **Sales**.

4. Right-click the Users container, point to New, and then select Group.

5. In the New Object – Group dialog box, type **New York Users** in the Group Name text box. Ensure that the Global option is selected under Group Scope and that the Distribution option is selected under Group Type. Click OK.

6. Right-click the Users container, point to New, and then select Group.

7. In the New Object – Group dialog box, type **International Marketing** in the Group Name text box. Ensure that the Universal option is selected under Group Scope and that the Security option is selected under Group Type. Click OK.

8. Right-click the Users container, point to New, and then select Group.

9. In the New Object – Group dialog box, type **International Sales** in the Group Name text box. Ensure that the Domain Local option is selected under Group Scope and that the Security option is selected under Group Type. Click OK.

10. When you are finished, use the Active Directory Users and Computers console to verify the creation of the following groups:

    ❑ International Marketing

    ❑ International Sales

    ❑ Marketing

    ❑ New York Users

    ❑ Sales

    > **QUESTION**   How can you quickly sort users from groups in the Active Directory Users and Computers console?

EXERCISE 4-4: MANAGING GROUP MEMBERSHIP

Estimated completion time: 10 minutes

The Human Resources department has asked that you add several new employees to some of the groups that you recently created for the department.

> **IMPORTANT** If you have two computers, complete the following tasks on Computerxx. If you are working with a partner, you and your lab partner should separately complete the following tasks on your designated computer.

1. In Active Directory Users and Computers, select the Users container.

2. In the details pane, right-click the Dan Holme user account created in Exercise 4-1 and select Add To A Group.

   The Select Group dialog box opens.

3. In the Select Group dialog box, type **Marketing** in the Enter The Object Name To Select text box.

   > **QUESTION** How are you able to get a list of all of the groups in the domain rather than having to type in the name?

4. Click OK.

5. Click OK to dismiss the message box informing you that the operation was successful.

6. Right-click the Dan Holme user account and click Add To A Group.

7. In the Select Group dialog box, type **International** in the Enter The Object Name To Select text box and then click OK.

   The Multiple Names Found dialog box opens.

8. In the Multiple Names Found dialog box, make sure International Marketing is selected and then click OK.

9. Click OK to dismiss the message box informing you that the operation was successful.

10. Open the Properties dialog box for the Dan Holme user account.

11. Select the Member Of tab as shown in Figure 4-3. Notice that the Dan Holme user account is now a member of both the Marketing and International Marketing groups as well as the Domain Users group. Once you have verified this, click OK.

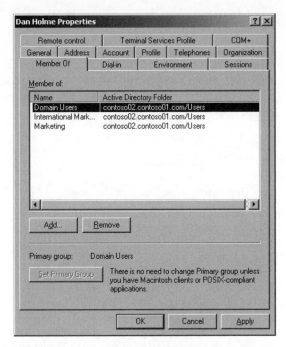

Figure 4-3   The Member Of tab of the Properties dialog box

12. Open the Properties dialog box for the Marketing global security group.

13. Select the Members tab and then click Add.

    The Select Users, Contacts, Computers, Or Groups dialog box opens.

14. Type **Sales** in the Enter The Object Names To Select text box. Click OK.

    Notice that the Sales global security group is now shown as a member of the Marketing global security group. This nesting arrangement—a global group added as a member of another global group—is possible only when the domain is configured to either the Windows Server 2003 or Windows 2000 native domain functional level.

15. Click OK to close the Properties dialog box.

EXERCISE 4-5: CHANGING GROUP TYPES AND SCOPES

Estimated completion time: 10 minutes

You have been asked to change the scope of the International Marketing group from universal to domain local. Originally, the group was supposed to be assigned rights but there was a mistake in the instructions you were handed. It is a Microsoft best practice to assign rights to domain local groups rather than universal groups.

> **IMPORTANT**   If you have two computers, complete the following tasks on Computerxx. If you are working with a partner, you and your lab partner should separately complete the following tasks on your designated computer.

To make this conversion, perform the following steps:

1. In Active Directory Users And Computers, right-click the Marketing global security group created in Exercise 4-3 and click Properties.

2. On the General tab, notice that the group scope can be changed only to universal and that the group type can be changed to distribution. Active Directory directory service does not allow global groups to be changed to domain local groups (or vice versa) under any circumstances. Click OK.

3. Open the Properties dialog box for the International Marketing universal security group.

4. On the General tab, notice that the group scope can be changed to either global or domain local. Select the Domain Local option and then click OK.

   The International Marketing group is now a domain local security group.

> **NOTE**   If Computeryy was not a global catalog server, step 4 would generate the following error message: "The following Active Directory error occurred: The requested operation can be performed only on a global catalog server."

EXERCISE 4-6: CONFIGURING ACCOUNT POLICIES

Estimated completion time: 10 minutes

The management of Contoso, Ltd., has determined that the network should be secured by locking out user accounts when those accounts are used to log on with invalid passwords. They have also directed you to audit such attempts.

> **IMPORTANT**   If you have two computers, complete the following tasks on Computerxx. If you are working with a partner, you and your lab partner should separately complete the following tasks on your designated computer.

1. In Active Directory Users And Computers, select the contosoxx.com (or contosoyy.contosoxx.com) node in the scope pane and open a Properties dialog box for the domain.

2. Select the Group Policy tab and then click Open to open the Group Policy Management console.

3. In the Group Policy Management console, right-click on the Default Domain policy and select Edit.

   The Group Policy Object Editor opens.

4. In the Group Policy Object Editor's scope pane, navigate to Computer Configuration\Windows Settings\Security Settings\Account Policies\Account Lockout Policy.

   > **QUESTION**   There are three policies available in the Account Lockout Policy node. What are the names of these policies and what do they do? (Right-click each policy and select help if you are unsure.)

5. Double-click the Account Lockout Duration policy.

   The policy's Properties dialog box opens.

6. Select the Define This Policy Setting check box.

7. Type **0** for the duration, then click Apply.

   The Suggested Value Changes dialog box opens, informing you that the Account Lockout Threshold and Reset Account Lockout Counter After policies will be configured with suggested values.

8. Click OK to confirm the settings, and then click OK to close the Properties dialog box.

9. In the Group Policy Object Editor's details pane, confirm that the Account Lockout Duration policy is set to zero, the Account Lockout Threshold policy is set to five invalid logon attempts, and the Reset Account Lockout Counter After policy is set to 30 minutes as shown in Figure 4-4.

   > **QUESTION**   Given the settings configured during this exercise, describe in your own words what would happen if someone entered the incorrect password more than five times in a 20-minute period. What if the wrong password was entered five times over a 40-minute period? What happens to the incorrect password counter if the correct password is entered?

10. Close the Group Policy Object Editor.

11. Close the Group Policy Management console.

12. Click OK to close the Properties dialog box for the domain.

13. In Active Directory Users and Computers, open the Properties dialog box for the Domain Controllers OU, under the domain node.

14. Select the Group Policy tab and then click Open to open the Group Policy Management console.

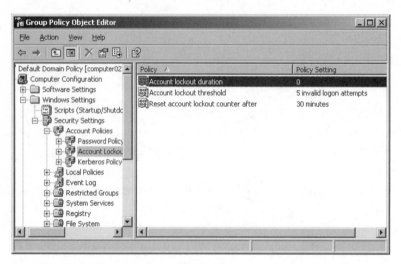

Figure 4-4   Account lockout policies

15. Right-click the Default Domain Controllers Policy, as shown in Figure 4-5 and select Edit.

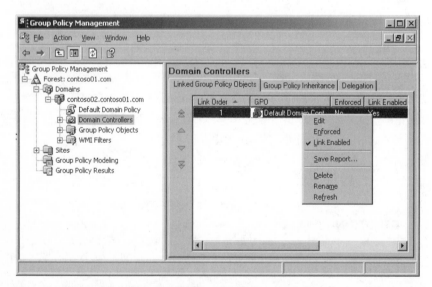

Figure 4-5   Right clicking on the Default Domain Controllers policy in the Group Policy Management console.

The Group Policy Object Editor opens.

16. Navigate to Computer Configuration\Windows Settings\Security Settings\Local Policies\Audit Policy.

17. Double-click the Audit Account Logon Events policy.

The policy's Properties dialog box opens.

18. Ensure the Define These Policy Settings check box is selected, and then select both the Success and Failure check boxes, and then click OK.

19. Double-click the Audit Logon Events policy.

The policy's Properties dialog box opens.

20. Ensure the Define These Policy Settings check box is selected, and then select both the Success and Failure check boxes, and then click OK.

> **QUESTION**   What happens when you audit for success and failure instead of just failure?

21. Close the Group Policy Object Editor.

22. Close the Group Policy Management console.

23. Click OK to close the Domain Controllers Properties dialog box.

24. Open a Command Prompt window, type **gpupdate /force**, and press ENTER.

A message in the console indicates that Group Policy refresh has occurred.

25. Close the command prompt.

EXERCISE 4-7: GENERATING AND EXAMINING LOGON EVENTS

Estimated completion time: 10 minutes

You now want to test that the system is recording logon events correctly. To do this you will use a user account to logon incorrectly twice and correctly once. Once you have done this you will search the log files to locate these events to check that they were recorded.

IMPORTANT   If you have two computers, complete the following tasks on Computerxx. If you are working with a partner, you and your lab partner should separately complete the following tasks on your designated computer.

1. In the scope pane of Active Directory Users and Computers, select the Users container.

2. In the details pane, right-click Rooslan Lee's user account and select Add To a Group.

   The Select Group dialog box opens.

3. Type **Server Operators** and click OK. Click OK in the success message box.

   NOTE   In order to log on to a domain controller, a user account must be a member of a group with the Allow Log On Locally user right for the domain controller. The Server Operators group has this right.

4. Close all open windows and log off the computer.

5. Generate two logon failure events for Rooslan Lee by attempting to log on twice to the computer with the username rlee and an invalid password.

6. Log on to the computer as Rooslan Lee. The user name is **rlee** and the password is the password you assigned in Exercise 4-1.

   QUESTION   Why were you asked to change the password when you logged on with this account for the first time?

7. Click OK, type in a new password and log on.

8. Log off the computer.

9. Log on to the computer as Administrator.

   QUESTION   Why do you have to log on as Administrator to view the security logs? What changes would have to be made to the Rooslan's account so that it could be used to view these logs?

10. Open the Event Viewer console from Administrative Tools.

11. Select the Security log.

12. Make sure the Category column is wide enough that you can identify the types of events that are logged.

13. Explore the events that have been generated by recent activity. Note the successful and failed logons. Figure 4-6 shows a logon failure event for Rooslan Lee.

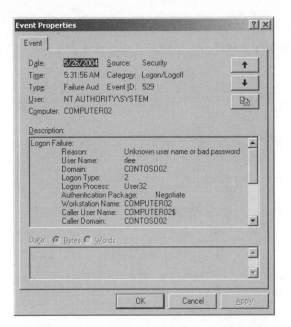

Figure 4-6   Logon failure event in Event Viewer

14. Close the Event Viewer console.

REVIEW QUESTIONS

Estimated completion time: 20 minutes

1. In your own words, describe what you learned during this lab.

2. When creating a user account, which of the following check-box options for passwords cannot be set at the same time?

❑ User Must Change Password At Next Logon

❑ User Cannot Change Password

❑ Password Never Expires

❑ Account Is Disabled

3. You are creating a user account for a new employee. How can you ensure that the employee does not have to change his or her password when first logging in?

4. You enable success/failure auditing of account logon events. Which event log should you check to see these events?

5. What is the term used for placing one group inside another group?

6. What types of authentication events are configured to be audited by default in the Default Domain Controllers policy?

LAB CHALLENGE 4-1: MODIFYING THE PROPERTIES OF MULTIPLE USER OBJECTS

Estimated completion time: 15 minutes

You have been asked by the Human Resources department to modify the attributes of several of the new users that you added accounts for earlier in the day. The HR department wants you to make the following changes:

■ The Orin Thomas, Rooslan Lee, Dan Holme, and Oksana Sitnikova accounts should have their Office listed as 127B.

■ The Orin Thomas, Rooslan Lee, Dan Holme, and Oksana Sitnikova accounts should expire at the end of December 31 of the current year.

■ The Orin Thomas, Rooslan Lee, Dan Holme, and Oksana Sitnikova accounts should have their Company field set to Contoso, Ltd.

■ The Orin Thomas, Rooslan Lee, Dan Holme, and Oksana Sitnikova accounts should have their logon hours set to allow logons only from 8 AM to 6 PM, Monday to Friday.

> **IMPORTANT**   If you have two computers, complete the following tasks on Computerxx. If you are working with a partner, you and your lab partner should separately complete the following tasks on your designated computer.

Without editing the properties of each of these accounts individually, how can you go about making these specific changes?

TROUBLESHOOTING LAB A
GROUP POLICY AND GROUP ADMINISTRATION

Troubleshooting Lab A is a practical application of the knowledge you have acquired from Labs 1 through 4. Your instructor or lab assistant has changed your computer configuration, causing it to "break." Your task in this lab will be to apply your acquired skills to troubleshoot and resolve the break. A scenario will be presented which will lay out the parameters of the break and the conditions that must be met for the scenario to be resolved. This troubleshooting lab has two break scenarios. The first break scenario involves Group Policy and the second break scenario involves groups.

> **NOTE   Do not proceed with this lab until you receive guidance from your instructor.**   The break scenario that you will be performing will depend on which computer you are using. The first computer will be Computerxx and the second computer will be Computeryy. Computerxx typically has an odd-numbered name, such as Computer01 and Computer03. Computeryy typically has an even-numbered name, such as Computer02 and Computer04 . If you are unsure of your computers name, run a command prompt and issue the **hostname** command. If you are using Computerxx, you will perform Break Scenario 1. If you are using Computeryy, you will perform Break Scenario 2. Your instructor or lab assistant may also have special instructions. Consult with your instructor before proceeding.

Break Scenario 1

> **IMPORTANT**   Perform this break scenario on Computerxx.

Contoso, Ltd. is a large accounting firm with offices in 20 cities. The company network contains five member servers running Windows Server 2003, Standard Edition, 200 client computers running Windows XP Professional, and three domain controllers running Windows Server 2003, Enterprise Edition. All computers are configured in a single, Active Directory site.

Company policy states that the Search menu and the Help menu should be removed from user's Start menu. Users should also be stopped from shutting down their Windows XP Professional computers using the Shut Down button located on the Start menu.

It has come to the attention of management that when two users, MarketingUser01 and MarketingUser02 log in, their Start menu is not in compliance with company policy. Management has asked you to determine the reason that these users Start menu does not comply and to resolve the problem so that the Search menu, Help menu, and Shut Down button are not present when they log in.

> **IMPORTANT**   For this exercise, each user is a member of the contosoxx.com domain and has the ability to log on locally to a domain controller. The password for each account is **P@ssw0rd**.

As you resolve the problem, fill out the worksheet in the TroubleshootingLabA folder and include the following information:

- Description of the problem.

- A list of all steps taken to diagnose the problem, even the ones that did not work.

- Description of the exact issue and solution.

- A list of the tools and resources you used to help solve this problem.

Break Scenario 2

> **IMPORTANT**   Perform this break scenario on Computeryy.

Contoso, Ltd. is a large accounting firm with offices in twenty cities. There are several Active Directory domains in the Contosoxx.com forest, all of which are child domains of Contosoxx.com.

Security and distribution groups are in use throughout the Contosoxx.com forest. Several administrators have recently been having problems managing these groups and have turned to you for a resolution for their problems. The administrators want to:

- Add the CONTOSOXX\TSA2-GRP2 group to the CONTOSOYY\TSA2-GRP4 group.

- Assign the CONTOSOYY\TSA2-GRP3 group NTFS full control (allow) permission to the C:\TSA2 folder.

- Ensure that the TSA2-GRP4 group is not a member of the TSA2-GRP5 group after group policy refreshes.

- Convert the TSA2-GRP6 group to a global security group. The current group membership does not need to be preserved.

As you resolve the problem, fill out the worksheet in the TroubleshootingLabA folder and include the following information:

- Description of the problem.

- A list of all steps taken to diagnose the problem, even the ones that did not work.

- Description of the exact issue and solution.

- A list of the tools and resources you used to help solve this problem.

LAB 5

REMOTE DESKTOP FOR ADMINISTRATION AND TERMINAL SERVER

Upon completion of this chapter, you will be able to:

- Exercise 5-1: Configuring the Server for Remote Desktop for Administration

- Exercise 5-2: Connecting to the Server with Remote Desktop Connection

- Exercise 5-3: Installing Terminal Server

- Exercise 5-4: Configuring Terminal Server Users

- Exercise 5-5: Connecting to Terminal Server and Checking Licensing

- Lab Review Questions

- Lab Challenge 5-1: Logging on to Terminal Server with Device Redirection

SCENARIO

You are a part of the Systems Administration team at Contoso, Ltd. Contoso, Ltd. has a large single-domain network with contoso.com as the domain root. You are responsible for the management of Contosos Ltd.'s Microsoft Windows Server 2003 computers. All of these computers are located in a secured server room in the datacenter at Contoso, Ltd.'s headquarters office building. Rather than logging on directly to these servers to perform administrative tasks, you will use the Remote Desktop for Administration features of Windows Server 2003 to perform these tasks from the comfort of your cubicle. Apart from the remote administration of servers located in the datacenter, Contoso, Ltd. wants you to explore the option of implementing Terminal Server as an alternative to installing applications on workstations.

After completing this lab, you will be able to:

- Configure a Windows Server 2003 computer so that a client can connect to it via Remote Desktop for Administration.

- Connect to a server via Remote Desktop Connection.

- Install Terminal Server on a Windows Server 2003 computer.

- Configure the properties of those users who connect to Terminal Server.

- Connect to Terminal Server and check licensing.

Estimated lesson time: 80 minutes

BEFORE YOU BEGIN

To successfully complete this lab, you will need the following:

- A computer with Windows Server 2003 installed and configured as a domain controller. (See Lab Exercises 2-1 and 2-2.)

- The computer should have its own domain, which will either be contoso*xx*.com or contoso*yy*.contoso*xx*.com.

- Have created the users Dan Holme and Orin Thomas (See Lab Exercise 4-1.)

> **NOTE** This lab is written to be performed on two computers. If each student has only a single computer, students can work as partners and share computers when needed. The first computer will be Computer*xx* and the second computer will be Computer*yy*. Computer*xx* typically has an odd-numbered name, such as Computer01 and Computer03. Computer*yy* typically has an even-numbered name, such as Computer02 and Computer04. If you are unsure of your computers name, run a command prompt and issue the **hostname** command.

EXERCISE 5-1: CONFIGURING A SERVER FOR REMOTE DESKTOP FOR ADMINISTATION

Estimated completion time: 10 minutes

Before you can access the servers in the datacenter from the comfort of your cubicle, you need to configure the servers to accept Remote Desktop for Administration connections. This involves logging on to the console (another way of saying sitting in front of the server with the keyboard and mouse) and making the appropriate configuration changes. You want to make sure that only one Remote Desktop for Administration connection can be used to a particular server at the same time. You also want to ensure that disconnected and idle sessions are automatically terminated. In the past, you've had a session disconnect and been unable to reconnect because the server believes the connection to be active. You then had to travel to the datacenter server room to manually terminate the session.

> **NOTE**   In this lab, you will use one Windows Server 2003 computer to connect to another Windows Server 2003 computer to make a Remote Desktop for Administration connection. In the real world you are more likely to be using a client such as Microsoft Windows XP Professional to make a Remote Desktop for Administration connection to Windows Server 2003.

> **IMPORTANT**   If you have two computers, complete the following tasks on Computerxx. If you are working with a partner, you and your lab partner should separately complete the following tasks on your designated computer. Some steps have computer-specific instructions.

1. Log on to the computer as Administrator. The password is P@ssw0rd or one assigned to you by your lab proctor. For Computerxx, select the contosoxx domain. For Computeryy, select the contosoyy domain.

2. Open System from Control Panel.

   The System Properties dialog box opens.

3. On the Remote tab, enable Remote Desktop for Administration by selecting the Allow Users To Connect Remotely To This Computer check box.

   A Remote Sessions message box appears indicating that remote connections must have passwords.

4. Click OK in the Remote Sessions message box.

> **QUESTION**   What other options can you set for Remote Desktop for Administration from the Remote tab of System Properties?

5. Click OK to close the System Properties dialog box.

6. Open the Terminal Services Configuration console from Administrative Tools.

7. In the Terminal Services Configuration console, right-click the RDP-Tcp connection in the details pane, and then click Properties.

The RDP-Tcp Properties dialog box opens.

8. On the Network Adapter tab, change the Maximum Connections: to **1**.

9. On the Sessions tab, select both of the Override User Settings check boxes, and specify the following settings as shown in Figure 5-1:

    ❑ End A Disconnected Session: 5 minutes

    ❑ Active Session Limit: Never

    ❑ Idle Session Limit: 5 minutes

    ❑ When Session Limit Is Reached Or Connection Is Broken: Disconnect From Session

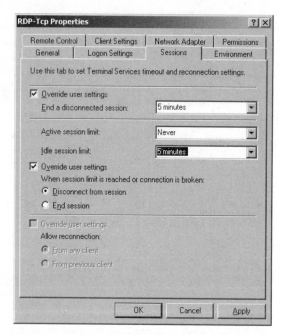

Figure 5-1 Terminal Services sessions settings

> **QUESTION** What are the four levels of Encryption available on the General Tab? Which is the most secure?

10. Click OK to close the RDP-Tcp Properties dialog box and close the Terminal Services Configuration console.

11. Open Active Directory Users And Computers.

12. In the Users container identify the accounts that you created in Lab 4 for Dan Holme and Orin Thomas. If you have forgotten the passwords that you assigned to these accounts, you should reset them.

13. Open the Properties dialog box for Dan Holme and Orin Thomas and clear the User Must Change Password At Next Logon checkbox on the Account tab.

14. If you are using Computerxx, add the Dan Holme account to the Administrators group. If you are using Computeryy, add the Orin Thomas account to the Administrators group.

15. Close Active Directory Users And Computers.

EXERCISE 5-2: CONNECTING TO A SERVER USING REMOTE DESKTOP CONNECTION

Estimated completion time: 5 minutes

Now that the server in the datacenter has been configured to accept Remote Desktop connections, it is time to check that connections can be established. You return to your cubicle and attempt to connect to the server in the datacenter.

> **IMPORTANT** If you have two computers, complete the following tasks on Computeryy. If you are working with a partner, you and your lab partner should separately complete the following tasks on your designated computer. Some steps have computer specific instructions.

1. Log on to the computer as Administrator.

2. Open Remote Desktop Connection (from All Programs\Accessories\Communications).

3. If you are using Computerxx, in the Computer box, type the name **computeryy.contosoyy.contosoxx.com** or IP address of Computeryy (which you determined in Lab 1), as shown in Figure 5-2. If you are using Computeryy, in the Computer box, type the name **computerxx.contosoxx.com** or IP address of Computerxx.

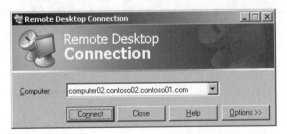

Figure 5-2 Remote Desktop Connection

4. Click Connect.

A tab title bar appears at the top of the screen. A Log On To Windows dialog box appears.

5. Log on to the computer. If you are using Computer*xx* to log into Computer*yy*, use the othomas account. If you are using Computer*yy* to log into Computer*xx*, use the dholme account. If the Manage Your Server dialog box appears, close it.

6. Open the Terminal Services Manager console in Administrative Tools.

You should see the remote session that you are currently using, indicated as session RDP-Tcp#1, as seen in Figure 5-3. Terminal Services Manager is used to manage remote connections, whether those sessions are using Remote Desktop for Administration or using Terminal Server, which we will be exploring in later exercises.

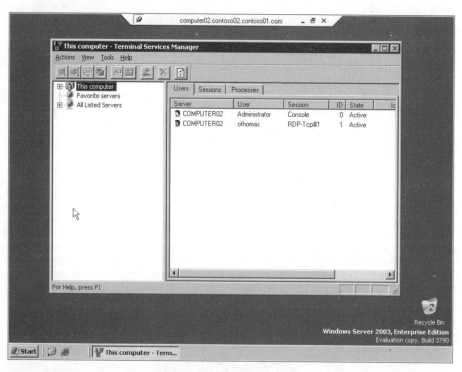

Figure 5-3   Terminal Services Manager showing an active Remote Desktop for Administration connection

7. In the Terminal Services Manager right-click the connection that you are using (either dholme or othomas) and select Status.

A Status Of LogonID dialog box opens. This dialog box shows network traffic details for the connection that you are using to connect one server to the other.

8. Click Close to close the Status Of LogonID dialog box.

9. If you have two computers, switch to Computer*xx*. If you are working with a partner, minimize the Remote Desktop Connection window by clicking the minimize button on the tab title bar.

10. Open Terminal Services Manager. If a message box appears that indicates that certain features work only when you run from a Terminal Server client session, click OK. You should now see the remote desktop connection.

11. Right-click the remote connection RDP-Tcp#1 and select Send Message.

    The Send Message dialog box opens.

12. In the Message box, type **Hello World**.

13. Click OK. The message should appear in Remote Desktop Connection window of the other computer as shown in Figure 5-4. Similarly, if you are working with a partner, the same message should appear in your Remote Desktop Connection window.

Figure 5-4   Message sent to a Remote Desktop for Administration session from Terminal Services Manager

> **QUESTION**   If other users were connected to this server via Terminal Server sessions at the same time, why might you send them a message via the Terminal Services Manager console?

> **QUESTION**   What happens if you leave the Remote Desktop Connection window open for more than 300 seconds without doing anything?

14. In the Remote Desktop Connection window, click Start and choose Log Off. In the Log Off Windows dialog box, click Log Off.

15. Close any open windows and log off both computers.

EXERCISE 5-3: INSTALLING TERMINAL SERVER

Estimated completion time: 20 minutes

Contoso, Ltd. is rolling out thin-client services to several of its departments. Rather than equip users with fully functional workstations, users will be connecting through the network to a Terminal Server on which they will be able to run applications such as Microsoft Office System. Terminals consist of little more than a monitor, keyboard, mouse, and a network card. Money is saved as the terminals are easier to maintain than client workstations and do not need to be regularly updated with patches and anti-virus software.

You will remember from Chapter 5 that Terminal Server is used to provide typical users access to applications on a remote Windows Server 2003 computer. Remote Desktop for Administration is used exclusively by administrators to perform maintenance and management tasks on a remote Windows Server 2003 computer. Remote Desktop for Administration allows up to two concurrent remote connections, while Terminal Server allows multiple concurrent remote connections that are limited by Terminal Server Licensing and server resources. Terminal Services is the underlying remote access technology that enables Remote Desktop for Administration and Terminal Server.

> **IMPORTANT**   If you have two computers, complete the following tasks on Computerxx. If you are working with a partner, you and your lab partner should separately complete the following tasks on your designated computer. Some steps have computer specific instructions.

1. Log on to the computer as Administrator.

2. Open Add Or Remove Programs from Control Panel.

3. Click Add/Remove Windows Components.

    The Windows Components Wizard opens.

4. If you are using Computerxx, select Terminal Server and Terminal Server Licensing. If you are using Computeryy, select only Terminal Server as shown in Figure 5-5

    A Configuration Warning appears reminding you that the Internet Explorer Enhanced Security Configuration will restrict users' Web access. As this Terminal Server will not be used primarily for Web access, this will not be a problem and installation should continue. Click Yes.

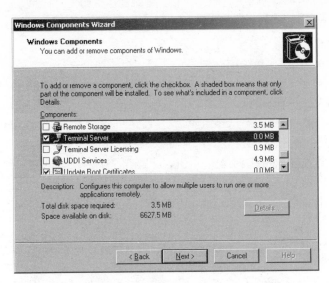

Figure 5-5 Installing the Terminal Server component

5. Click Next. A message appears explaining the installation of applications on a Terminal Server and licensing. Read the message carefully.

> **QUESTION** To enable non-Administrator users to access the Terminal Server, what do you need to do with their user accounts?

> **QUESTION** What does the message warn will happen to programs that are currently installed on the server?

6. Click Next. Application compatibility security options appear.

> **QUESTION** Which level of application compatibility security would you select if your Terminal Server is hosting an application written for Microsoft Windows NT 4.0?

7. Ensure that Full Security is selected and click Next.

8. If you are using Computerxx, the Terminal Server Licensing Setup page appears. Ensure that the Your Entire Enterprise option is selected and click Next. If you are using Computeryy, installation will occur without step 8.

   You might be asked to insert your Windows Server 2003 CD-ROM.

9. When installation finishes, click Finish.

   A System Settings Change message box appears indicating that the computer needs to be restarted.

10. Click Yes to restart the computer.

EXERCISE 5-4: CONFIGURING TERMINAL SERVER USERS

Estimated completion time: 5 minutes

As part of the Terminal Server test deployment, you have selected several normal users from the accounting department to trial the technology. They will report back to you about their experiences, helping you further refine how Terminal Server will be introduced to the wider user base at Contoso, Ltd. Before this occurs, the normal users who will be testing this technology need to have accounts created. These accounts also need to be configured so that the users are able to log onto a Windows Server 2003 computer running Terminal Server.

> **IMPORTANT**   If you have two computers, complete the following tasks on Computerxx. If you are working with a partner, you and your lab partner should separately complete the following tasks on your designated computer. Some steps have computer specific instructions.

1. Log on to the computer as Administrator.

2. Open the Group Policy Management console.

3. Expand the Domain Controllers node, right click on the Default Domain Controller policy and select Edit.

   The Group Policy Object Editor opens.

4. Open the Computer Configuration\Windows Settings\Security Settings\Local Policies\User Rights Assignment node.

5. Open the properties dialog box for the Allow Log On Through Terminal Services policy. If you are using Computerxx, add the user Orin Thomas to this policy. If you are using Computeryy, add the user Dan Holme to this policy.

6. Close the Group Policy Object Editor and close the Group Policy Management console.

7. Open Active Directory Users and Computers. If you are using Computerxx, add the user Orin Thomas to the Remote Desktop Users group. If you are using Computeryy, add the user Dan Holme to the Remote Desktop Users group.

8. Close Active Directory Users and Computers.

9. Open a Command Prompt window and issue the command **gpupdate /force**.

IMPORTANT   We performed this exercise because both lab computers are domain controllers. Terminal Servers are almost always member servers. To give a user access to a Terminal Server you typically just add them to the local Remote Desktop Users group.

EXERCISE 5-5: CONNECTING TO TERMINAL SERVER AND CHECKING LICENSING

Estimated completion time: 5 minutes

As part of the Terminal Server test deployment, you have selected several normal users from the accounting department to trial the technology. You want to check now that these users are able to connect to Terminal Server and can activate the Wordpad application. At present, Wordpad will be a substitute for the Microsoft Office System applications that you will install later. You also wish to check that Terminal Server licensing is functioning correctly.

IMPORTANT   If you have two computers, complete the following tasks on Computeryy. If you are working with a partner, you and your lab partner should separately complete the following tasks on your designated computer. Some steps have computer specific instructions.

1. Log on to the computer as Administrator.

2. Open Remote Desktop Connection. If you are using Computerxx, connect to computeryy.contosoyy.contosoxx.com and log in using the dholme account. If you are using Computeryy, connect to computerxx.contosoxx.com and log in using the othomas account.

3. Run the Wordpad application and then log off the Terminal Server connection.

4. On Computerxx, open the Terminal Server Licensing console.

5. In the console, check how many Temporary Licenses for Windows Server 2003 have been issued. You do not need to activate the license server to perform this function.

REVIEW QUESTIONS

Estimated completion time: 20 minutes

1. In your own words, describe what you learned during this lab.

2. What is the difference between Remote Desktop for Administration and Terminal Server?

3. Why should you consider setting an idle timeout for Terminal Server sessions?

4. What is the difference between an active session limit and an idle session limit?

5. What tool would you use to forcibly disconnect three users that are connected to Terminal Server so that you can perform maintenance on the computer?

6. As described when installing Terminal Server, what special action must be taken to install an application that will be shared, such as Microsoft Office, on a Terminal Server?

LAB CHALLENGE 5-1: LOGGING ON TO TERMINAL SERVER WITH DEVICE REDIRECTION

Estimated completion time: 15 minutes

You wish to configure the Terminal Server connection so that the local workstation's hard disk drives are available from the My Computer icon when logged into the Terminal Server. As you don't have access to the workstation, you will be performing this on the two Terminal Servers that you have configured.

> **IMPORTANT**   If you have two computers, complete the following tasks on Computeryy. If you are working with a partner, you and your lab partner should separately complete the following tasks on your designated computer. Some steps have computer specific instructions.

- Log on to the computer as Administrator.

- Use the Remote Desktop Connection options to have the local hard disk visible on the remote computer.

- If you are using Computerxx, log on to Computeryy using the dholme account. If you are using Computeryy, log on to Computerxx using the othomas account.

- Provide a screenshot for your instructor displaying the My Computer window.

LAB 6
USING AUTOMATION FOR USER AND GROUP ACCOUNTS

This lab contains the following exercises and activities:

Upon completion of this chapter, you will be able to:

- ■ Exercise 6-1: Managing User Accounts from the Command Line

- ■ Exercise 6-2: Managing Group Accounts from the Command Line

- ■ Exercise 6-3: Importing and Exporting User Accounts with Csvde

- ■ Exercise 6-4: Importing and Exporting User Accounts with Ldifde

- ■ Exercise 6-5: Using Scripts to Automate Administration

- ■ Review Questions

- ■ Lab Challenge 6-1: Listing Groups and Group Members

- ■ Lab Challenge 6-2: Modifying User Properties

- ■ Lab Challenge 6-3: Managing Users and Groups Using Scripts

SCENARIO

You are a part of the domain Administration team at Contoso, Ltd. Contoso, Ltd. has a large single-domain network with contoso.com as the domain root. You are responsible for the management of user and group accounts within the contoso.com domain. Contoso, Ltd. has recently migrated to Microsoft Windows Server 2003 and your team leader has asked you to explore ways that the management of users and groups can be automated to make the process more efficient. Specifically you have been asked to explore how to:

After completing this lab, you will be able to:

- Add and modify user accounts from the command line.

- Add and modify group accounts from the command line.

- Search and find information about user accounts from the command line.

- Use query-based criteria as input for other command-line-based tools.

- Import and export user account information.

- Use VBScript files to automate Active Directory administration.

Estimated lesson time: 110 minutes

BEFORE YOU BEGIN

To successfully complete this lab, you will need to have completed the following labs:

- A computer with Windows Server 2003 installed and configured as a domain controller. (See Lab Exercises 2-1 and 2-2.)

- The computer should have its own domain, which will either be named contoso*xx*.com or contoso*yy*.contoso*xx*.com.

- The domain functional level must be set to Windows 2000 native or Windows Server 2003. (See Lab Challenge 2-1).

- Installed the Group Policy Management console. (See Lab Exercise 3-1)

> **NOTE**   This lab is written to be performed on two computers. If each student has only a single computer, students can work as partners and share computers when needed. The first computer will be Computer*xx* and the second computer will be Computer*yy*. Computer*xx* typically has an odd-numbered name, such as Computer01 and Computer03. Computer*yy* typically has an even-numbered name, such as Computer02 and Computer04. If you are unsure of your computers name, run a command prompt and issue the **hostname** command.

EXERCISE 6-1: MANAGING USER ACCOUNTS FROM THE COMMAND LINE

Estimated completion time: 15 minutes

The Contoso, Ltd. domain has five top-level OUs: Accounting, IT, Managers, Marketing, and Sales. You need to add users and groups as well as to modify certain properties for various users and groups for Contoso, Ltd. One new user needs to be added to the Accounting OU and three new users need to be added to the Sales OU. You also have been asked to determine of which groups Susan Burk is a member.

> **IMPORTANT**   If you have two computers, complete the following tasks on Computerxx. If you are working with a partner, you and your lab partner can separately complete the following tasks on your designated computer.

1. Log on to the computer as Administrator. Your username is **Administrator**. The password is P@ssw0rd. For Computerxx, select the contosoxx domain. For Computeryy, select the contosoyy domain.

2. Open the Active Directory Users and Computers console and create the following first-level OUs: Accounting, IT, Managers, Marketing, and Sales.

3. Click Start, click Run, type the command **cmd**, and press Enter. A command-prompt window appears.

4. Add new user #1, John Smith, to the Accounting OU by typing the following command all on one line in the command-prompt window and then pressing ENTER. Be sure to replace *xx* or *yy* with the appropriate computer number.

   ```
   dsadd user "CN=John Smith,OU=Accounting,DC=Contosoxx,DC=Com" –UPN
   John.Smith@contosoxx.com –SAMID Jsmith –FN John –LN Smith –PWD 452~wwwTT
   –HMDIR \\computerxx\users\jsmith –HMDRV h:
   ```

   > **NOTE**   If you are completing this lab using Computeryy, make the following substitutions when prompted to type in commands. Sample input and output for Computeryy is shown in Figure 6-1 at the end of this exercise.
   >
   > Change: DC=contosoxx To: DC=contosoyy,DC=contosoxx
   >
   > Change: @contosoxx.com To: @contosoyy.contosoxx.com
   >
   > Change: computerxx To: computeryy

   > **NOTE**   If you typed the command correctly, the Dsadd command displays the following output:
   >
   > dsadd succeeded:CN=John Smith,OU=Accounting,DC=contosoxx,DC=com

5. Check the results of adding John Smith as a new user within the Accounting OU in the Active Directory Users and Computers console. You may need to refresh the display by pressing the F5 key.

6. Add new user #2, Kelly Focht, to the Sales OU by typing the following command all on one line at a command-prompt window:

```
dsadd user "CN=Kelly Focht,OU=Sales,DC=Contosoxx,DC=Com" -UPN
Kelly.Focht@contosoxx.com -SAMID KFocht -FN Kelly -LN Focht -PWD
971sssBBB -TEL 888-111-2233 -FAX 888-111-4477
```

> **NOTE** If you typed the command correctly, the Dsadd command displays the following output:
>
> ```
> dsadd succeeded:CN=Kelly Focht,OU=Sales,DC=contoso,DC=com
> ```

7. Check the results of adding Kelly Focht as a new user within the Sales OU in the Active Directory Users and Computers console. Refresh the display by pressing the F5 key.

8. Add new user #3, John Arthur, to the Sales OU by typing the following command all on one line at a command-prompt window:

```
dsadd user "CN=John Arthur,OU=Sales,DC=Contosoxx,DC=Com" -UPN
John.Arthur@contosoxx.com -SAMID JArthur -FN John -LN Arthur -PWD
$$$bag555 -MEMBEROF "CN=server operators,CN=builtin,DC=Contosoxx,
DC=Com" "CN=account operators,CN=builtin,DC=Contosoxx,DC=com"
```

> **NOTE** If you typed the command correctly, the Dsadd command displays the following output:
>
> ```
> dsadd succeeded:CN=John Arthur,OU=Sales,DC=contoso,DC=com
> ```

9. Check the results of adding John Arthur as a new user within the Sales OU in the Active Directory Users and Computers console. Refresh the display by pressing the F5 key.

10. Add new user #4, Susan Burk, to the Managers OU by typing the following command all on one line at a command-prompt window:

```
dsadd user "CN=Susan Burk,OU=Managers,DC=Contosoxx,DC=Com" -UPN
Susan.Burk@contosoxx.com -SAMID SBurk -FN Susan -LN Burk -PWD $$$Bo$$$
-MEMBEROF "CN=server operators,CN=builtin,DC=Contosoxx,DC=Com"
"CN=account operators,CN=builtin,DC=Contosoxx,DC=com" "CN=backup
operators,CN=builtin,DC=Contosoxx,DC=Com" "CN=Domain Admins,
CN=Users,DC=Contosoxx,DC=Com"
```

> **NOTE** If you typed the command correctly, the Dsadd command displays the following output:
>
> ```
> dsadd succeeded:CN=Susan Burk,OU=Managers,DC=contoso,DC=com
> ```

11. To find out which groups that Susan Burk belongs to, type the following command all on one line at a command prompt:

```
dsget user "CN=Susan Burk,OU=Managers,DC=Contosoxx,DC=Com" -memberof
```

NOTE   If you typed the command correctly, the Dsget command displays the following output:

`"CN=Account Operators,CN=Builtin,DC=contosoxx,DC=com"`

`"CN=Server Operators,CN=Builtin,DC=contosoxx,DC=com"`

`"CN=Domain Admins,CN=Users,DC=contosoxx,DC=com"`

`"CN=Backup Operators,CN=Builtin,DC=contosoxx,DC=com"`

`"CN=Domain Users,CN=Users,DC=contosoxx,DC=com"`

Figure 6-1   Sample input and output on Computer*yy*.

EXERCISE 6-2: MANAGING GROUP ACCOUNTS FROM THE COMMAND LINE

Estimated completion time: 20 minutes

For your next task, you need to create two new groups based on the properties and property values listed in the following tables. You also need to search through groups to determine which groups are global in scope. Finally, by using the Dsquery command as an input pipe, you will modify the Sales group with the Dsmod command so that it becomes a distribution group type instead of a security group type.

Properties for New Group #1	Property Values
Group Name	Sales Managers
SAM Name (pre-Windows 2000)	Sales Managers
Container or Organizational Unit	Sales
Group Type	Security
Group Scope	Global

Properties for New Group #1	Property Values
Members	Kelly Focht, John Arthur
Member of	Remote Desktop Users; Backup Operators

Properties for New Group #2	Property Values
Group Name	IT Staff
SAM Name (pre-Windows 2000)	IT Staff
Container or Organizational Unit	IT
Group Type	Security
Group Scope	Global
Members	Administrator, Susan Burk
Member of	Remote Desktop Users; Server Operators

IMPORTANT If you have two computers, complete the following tasks on Computerxx. If you are working with a partner, you and your lab partner can separately complete the following tasks on your designated computer.

1. Open a command prompt.

2. Add new group #1, Sales Managers, to the Sales OU by typing the following command all on one line in the command-prompt window:

```
dsadd group "CN=Sales Managers,OU=Sales,DC=Contosoxx,DC=Com" –SAMID
"Sales Managers" –SECGRP yes –SCOPE g –MEMBERS "CN=Kelly Focht,
OU=Sales,DC=Contosoxx,DC=Com" "CN=John Arthur,OU=Sales,DC=Contosoxx,
DC=Com" –MEMBEROF "CN=Remote Desktop Users,CN=Builtin,DC=Contosoxx,
DC=Com" "CN=Backup Operators,CN=Builtin,DC=Contosoxx,DC=Com"
```

NOTE If you are completing this lab using Computeryy, make the following substitutions when prompted to type in commands.

```
Change: DC=contosoxx To: DC=contosoyy,DC=contosoxx
```

NOTE If you typed the command correctly, the Dsadd command displays the following output:

```
dsadd succeeded:CN=Sales Managers,OU=Sales,DC=contosoxx,DC=com
```

3. Open the Active Directory Users and Computers console.

4. Verify that you have added Sales Managers as a new global security group within the Sales OU in the Active Directory Users and Computers console.

> **NOTE**   You may need to refresh the display by pressing the F5 key. Kelly Focht and John Arthur should be members of the group and the Sales Managers group should be a member of the Backup Operators group and the Remote Desktop Users group.

5. Add new group #2, IT Staff, to the IT OU by typing the following command all on one line at a command-prompt window:

```
dsadd group "CN=IT Staff,OU=IT,DC=Contosoxx,DC=Com" -SAMID "IT Staff"
-SECGRP yes -SCOPE g -MEMBERS "CN=Administrator,CN=Users,DC=Contosoxx,
DC=Com" "CN=Susan Burk,OU=Managers,DC=Contosoxx,DC=Com" -MEMBEROF
"CN=Remote Desktop Users,CN=Builtin,DC=Contosoxx,DC=Com" "CN=Server
Operators,CN=Builtin,DC=Contosoxx,DC=Com"
```

> **NOTE**   If you typed the command correctly, the Dsadd command displays the following output:

```
dsadd succeeded:CN=IT Staff,OU=IT,DC=contosoxx,DC=com
```

6. Open the Active Directory Users and Computers console.

7. Verify that you have added IT Staff as a new global security group within the IT OU in the Active Directory Users and Computers console.

> **NOTE**   You may need to refresh the display by pressing the F5 key. Administrator and Susan Burk should be members of the group and the IT Staff group should be a member of the Server Operators group and the Remote Desktop Users group.

8. Determine which group names within the domain begin with the letter "s" by typing the following command all on one line at a command prompt:

```
dsquery group -NAME s*
```

> **QUESTION**   Which group names begin with the letter "s"?

9. Use the Dsquery command to specify which group(s) that begin with the letters "sa" should be changed to a distribution group type as an input parameter for the Dsmod command. In addition, specify on the command line that you want to add John Smith as a member to each of the qualifying groups. Type the following command all on one line at a command prompt:

```
dsquery group -NAME sa* | dsmod group -SECGRP no -ADDMBR "CN=John
Smith,OU=Accounting,DC=Contosoxx,DC=Com"
```

10. From the Active Directory Users and Computers console, verify that the Sales Managers group is now a distribution group type and that you have added the user John Smith from the Accounting OU as a member of this group. (If you created a Sales group in Lab 4, the same change will also be applied to the Sales group.)

> **NOTE** John Arthur, John Smith, and Kelly Focht now should all be members of the Sales Managers group.

EXERCISE 6-3: IMPORTING AND EXPORTING USER ACCOUNTS WITH CSVDE

Estimated completion time: 10 minutes

Your manager instructs you to import two user accounts into the Marketing OU for the domain using data from the NewUsers.csv file. After you perform the import procedure, you have been requested to export the user and group accounts stored in the Sales OU into a new file named SalesUsers.csv.

> **IMPORTANT** If you have two computers, complete the following tasks on Computerxx. If you are working with a partner, you and your lab partner can separately complete the following tasks on your designated computer.

1. Open the Notepad text editor.

2. In Notepad, type the following three lines of text. (An indented line is a continuation of the previous line.)

```
DN,objectClass,sAMAccountName,sn,givenName,userPrincipalName
"CN=Dan Bacon,OU=Marketing,DC=contosoxx,DC=com",
 user,dbacon,Bacon,Dan,dan.bacon@contosoxx.com
"CN=Larry Zhang,OU=Marketing,DC=contosoxx,DC=com",
 user,lzhang,Zhang,Larry,larry.zhang@contosoxx.com
```

> **NOTE** If you are completing this lab using Computeryy, make the following substitutions when prompted to type in commands.
>
> Change: DC=contosoxx To: DC=contosoyy,DC=contosoxx
>
> Change: @contosoxx.com To: @contosoyy.contosoxx.com

3. Close Notepad and click Yes when prompted to save the file. Save the file as "**C:\NewUsers.csv**" (be sure to include the quotes).

4. Open a command prompt and type the following command:

```
csvde -i -f c:\newusers.csv
```

> **NOTE** If you typed the listing correctly, the Csvde command should display the following output:
>
> ```
> Connecting to "<null>"
>
> Logging in as current user using SSPI
>
> Importing directory from file "c:\newusers.csv"
>
> Loading entries...
>
> 2 entries modified successfully.
>
> The command has completed successfully.
> ```

5. Open the Active Directory Users and Computers console to verify that the two new users were successfully imported into the Marketing OU.

> **QUESTION** Are these two new users enabled?

6. Go to the command prompt again and type the following command to export all the current users and groups contained in the Sales OU into a .csv file:

```
csvde -m -f c:\salesusers.csv -d "OU=sales,DC=contosoxx,DC=com"
```

> **NOTE** If you typed the command correctly, the Csvde command should display the following output:
>
> ```
> Connecting to "<null>"
>
> Logging in as current user using SSPI
>
> Exporting directory to file "c:\salesusers.csv"
>
> Searching for entries...
>
> Writing out entries...
>
> Export completed. Post-processing in progress...
>
> 4 entries exported
>
> The command has completed successfully
> ```

7. Open the C:\SalesUsers.csv file in Notepad, shown in figure 6-2, to verify that the users and groups from the Sales OU were successfully exported. Turn on word wrap to view the file more easily.

Figure 6-2   SalesUsers.csv containing exported user and group accounts in Sales OU

EXERCISE 6-4: IMPORTING AND EXPORTING USER ACCOUNTS WITH LDIFDE

Estimated completion time: 15 minutes

Now your manager asks you to export all of the user and group accounts contained within the Sales OU, but he needs the export file to be formatted using the LDAP Data Interchange Format. After you perform the export procedure, you also have been requested to import two new groups into the IT OU using a file named ImportGroups.ldf.

> **IMPORTANT**   If you have two computers, complete the following tasks on Computerxx. If you are working with a partner, you and your lab partner can separately complete the following tasks on your designated computer.

1. In a command prompt and type the following command to export all the current users and groups contained in the Sales OU into an .ldf file:

```
ldifde –m –f c:\exportsales.ldf –d "OU=sales,DC=contosoxx,DC=com"
```

> **NOTE**   If you are completing this lab using Computeryy, make the following substitutions when prompted to type in commands.
>
> Change: DC=contosoxx To: DC=contosoyy,DC=contosoxx

NOTE If you typed the command correctly, the Ldifde command should display the following output:

```
Connecting to "computerxx.contosoxx.com"

Logging in as current user using SSPI

Exporting directory to file "c:\exportsales.ldf"

Searching for entries...

Writing out entries...

4 entries exported

The command has completed successfully
```

2. Open the C:\ExportSales.ldf file in Notepad to verify that the users and groups from the Sales OU were successfully exported and then close Notepad.

3. Open Notepad to create a new text file for importing two new groups in the domain using Ldifde.

4. In the Notepad window, type the following text:

```
DN: CN=HelpDesk,OU=IT,DC=Contosoxx,DC=Com

changeType: add

CN: HelpDesk

description: HelpDesk Staff

objectClass: group

sAMAccountName: HelpDesk


DN: CN=Technicians,OU=IT,DC=Contosoxx,DC=Com

changeType: add

CN: Technicians

description: Technical Personnel

objectClass: group

sAMAccountName: Technicians
```

5. Close Notepad and click Yes when prompted to save the file. Save the file as "**C:\ImportGroups.ldf**" (be sure to include the quotes).

6. Open a command prompt and type the following command:

```
ldifde -i -f c:\importgroups.ldf
```

NOTE If you typed the listing correctly, the Ldifde command should display the following output:

```
Connecting to "computerxx.contosoxx.com"

Logging in as current user using SSPI

Importing directory from file "c:\importusers.ldf"

Loading entries...

2 entries exported successfully

The command has completed successfully
```

7. Open the Active Directory Users and Computers console to verify that the two new groups (HelpDesk and Technicians) were successfully imported into the IT OU.

> **QUESTION**   What are their group types and group scope?

EXERCISE 6-5: USING SCRIPTS TO AUTOMATE ADMINISTRATION

Estimated completion time: 15 minutes

Contoso, Ltd., is about to hire 500 new employees. You will be in charge of adding all of those new users to the Contosoxx.com domain and placing them into their appropriate groups and OUs. Management has read a trade publication that suggests that scripts for Microsoft Windows Script Host is the most efficient way to create and configure the new users and groups that will be required. Your manager wants you to investigate whether or not what they have read in the publication is actually true. The selected scripting language is Microsoft Visual Basic Scripting Edition (VBScript).

> **IMPORTANT**   If you have two computers, complete the following tasks on Computerxx. If you are working with a partner, you and your lab partner can separately complete the following tasks on your designated computer.

1. Open Notepad and type the following code.

```
Set objOU = GetObject("LDAP://OU=Marketing,dc=contosoxx,dc=com")

Set objGroup = objOU.Create("Group", "cn=Copy Writers")

objGroup.Put "sAMAccountName", "Copy Writers"

objGroup.SetInfo
```

> **NOTE**   If you are completing this lab using Computeryy, make the following substitutions when prompted to type in commands.
>
> Change: DC=contosoxx To: DC=contosoyy,DC=contosoxx

2. Close Notepad and save the file as "**C:\AddGroup.vbs**" (be sure to include the quotes).

3. Open a command prompt, type **C:\AddGroup.vbs**, and press Enter to run the script.

> **NOTE**   You should not see any error message displayed after running the command. If one or more errors display, check each line of the script to make sure that you have typed it correctly.

4. Open the Active Directory Users and Computers console to verify that the new group Copy Writers was successfully created in the Marketing OU.

5. Open Notepad and type the following code (the underscore is a line continuation character).

```
Set objGroup = GetObject _

  ("LDAP://cn=Copy Writers,OU=Marketing,dc=contosoxx,dc=com")

objGroup.Add "LDAP://cn=Susan Burk,OU=Managers,dc=contosoxx,dc=com"
```

6. Close Notepad and save the file as "**C:\AddUserToGroup.vbs**" (be sure to include the quotes).

7. Open a command prompt, type **C:\AddUserToGroup.vbs**, and press Enter to run the script.

> **NOTE**   You should not see any error message displayed after running the command. If one or more errors display, check each line of the script to make sure that you have typed it correctly.

8. Open the Active Directory Users and Computers console to verify that Susan Burk was added successfully to the Copy Writers group.

9. Open Notepad and type the following code.

```
Set objOU = GetObject("LDAP://OU=Marketing,dc=contosoxx,dc=com")

Set objUser = objOU.Create("User", "cn=Mary Baker")

objUser.Put "sAMAccountName", "Mary.Baker"

objUser.SetInfo
```

10. Close Notepad and save the file as "**C:\AddUser.vbs**" (be sure to include the quotes).

11. Open a command prompt, type **C:\AddUser.vbs**, and press Enter to run the script.

NOTE You should not see any error message displayed after running the command. If one or more errors display, check each line of the script to make sure that you have typed it correctly.

12. Open the Active Directory Users and Computers console to verify that the new user Mary Baker was successfully created in the Marketing OU.

REVIEW QUESTIONS

Estimated completion time: 10 minutes

1. In your own words, describe what you learned during this lab.

2. Which command-line tool(s) can import users and groups into Active Directory, export users and groups from Active Directory, and make changes the properties of existing users and groups?

3. What is the status of user accounts created using Csvde, Ldifde, or a script file?

4. Type the following command at a command prompt and press Enter:

   `Dsquery group "CN=Builtin,DC=Contosoxx,DC=Com"`

   What does this command do and what are its results?

5. Type the following command at a command prompt and press Enter:

   `Dsquery group "CN=Builtin,DC=Contosoxx,DC=Com" | dsget group -members`

   What does this command do and what are its results?

LAB CHALLENGE 6-1: LISTING GROUPS AND GROUP MEMBERS

Estimated completion time: 10 minutes

As a senior network administrator, you want to continue to streamline user and group account management using available command-line tools and Windows Script Host programming features. You want to list all groups in the Built-in container of Active Directory as well as the members of those groups. You also want to save the results to a text file named BuiltinGroupsMembers.txt. Using a command-line solution, how would you do this?

LAB CHALLENGE 6-2: MODIFYING USER PROPERTIES

Estimated completion time: 10 minutes

User accounts created in earlier in Exercise 6-3 are disabled. You want to enable all the accounts in the Marketing OU. Using a command-line solution, how would you do this?

LAB CHALLENGE 6-3: MANAGING USERS AND GROUPS USING SCRIPTS

Estimated completion time: 15 minutes

You want to create two new global security groups in the Sales OU:

- Staff

- Team Leaders

You want to create two new users in the new Sales OU:

- Lori Oviatt

- Bridgette Lloyd

And you want to add the two new users to the two new groups.

Based on the code from this lab, write VBScript code to create the new groups, create the new users, and then add the new users to the new groups. Save the VBScript code in three separate files: CreateGroups.vbs, CreateUsers.vbs, and AddUsersToGroups.vbs.

INTERNET INFORMATION SERVICES

- Exercise 7-1: Installing IIS

- Exercise 7-2: Creating a New Web Site

- Exercise 7-3: Creating a Secure Virtual Directory

- Exercise 7-4: Setting Up an FTP Server for Access by Only a Specific Group of Users

- Review Questions

- Lab Challenge 7-1: Locking Down IIS So That It Can be Accessed Only from a Specific IP Address.

SCENARIO

Contoso, Ltd., would like to migrate from its current Web-hosting solution to start using Microsoft Internet Information Services (IIS) included with Microsoft Windows Server 2003. Contoso, Ltd., will be using these services primarily for Web hosting though management has mentioned the idea of setting up an FTP server as a place for remote users to upload files.

After completing this lab, you will be able to:

- **Install IIS on Windows Server 2003.**

- **Create a basic Web site using the IIS Manager snap-in.**

- **Secure IIS so that only authorized users are able to access particular content.**

- **Configure an FTP site so that only certain users can access content.**

Estimated lesson time: 70 minutes

BEFORE YOU BEGIN

To successfully complete this lab, you will need to have completed the following labs:

- A computer with Windows Server 2003 installed and configured as a domain controller. (See Lab Exercises 2-1 and 2-2.)

- The computer should have its own domain, which will either be named contosoxx.com or contosoyy.contosoxx.com.

   > **NOTE**   This lab is written to be performed on two computers. If each student has only a single computer, students can work as partners and share computers when needed. The first computer will be Computerxx and the second computer will be Computeryy. Computerxx typically has an odd-numbered name, such as Computer01 and Computer03. Computeryy typically has an even-numbered name, such as Computer02 and Computer04 . If you are unsure of your computers name, run a command prompt and issue the **hostname** command.

EXERCISE 7-1: INSTALLING IIS

Estimated completion time: 10 minutes

The first step in Contoso, Ltd.'s, plan to run IIS is to install it on a server on the pilot network. The domain controller on the pilot network has been chosen to host IIS, though once the pilot program has concluded, IIS will be deployed to a server that is dedicated to this task.

   > **IMPORTANT**   If you have two computers, complete the following tasks on Computerxx. If you are working with a partner, you and your lab partner should separately complete the following tasks on your designated computer.

Installing IIS

1. Log on to the computer as Administrator. Your username is **Administrator**. The password is P@ssw0rd. For Computerxx, select the contosoxx domain. For Computeryy, select the contosoyy domain.

2. Open Add Or Remove Programs from the Control Panel and click Add/Remove Windows Components.

   The Windows Components Wizard opens.

3. Select Application Server and click Details.

The Application Server dialog box opens.

4. Select Internet Information Services (IIS) and click Details.

The Internet Information Services (IIS) dialog box opens.

5. Ensure that, at a minimum, Common Files, File Transfer Protocol (FTP) Service, Internet Information Services Manager, and World Wide Web Service are selected as shown in Figure 7-1.

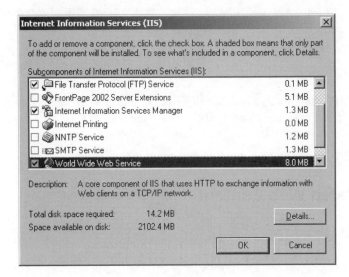

Figure 7-1   Components of Internet Information Services

> **QUESTION**   *Create a list of all the components that can be installed with IIS and describe their function.*

6. Click OK twice and then click Next in the Windows Components Wizard to install IIS and its components. (You might be asked to insert your Windows Server 2003 CD.)

7. When installation completes, click Finish.

Setting Up Accounts

The following steps create a WEBUser account and a FTPUsers group that will be used for exercises later in this lab. These steps are not necessary when installing IIS.

1. Open the Active Directory Users And Computers console.

2. In the Users container, create a new user named WEBUser. Set the password to P@ssw0rd and clear the User Must Change Password At Next Logon check box. (For information on creating users and groups, see Lab 4.)

3. In the Users container, create a new domain local security group named FTPUsers.

EXERCISE 7-2: CREATING A NEW WEB SITE

Estimated completion time: 10 minutes

The marketing department of Contoso, Ltd., is in the process of designing a Web site that reflects the company's needs and interests. As it will be some time before Contoso, Ltd., management approves the design, you wish to get a pilot site up and running so that you can implement other features such as Web site security. To do this, take the following steps:

> **IMPORTANT**   If you have two computers, complete the following tasks on Computerxx. If you are working with a partner, you and your lab partner should separately complete the following tasks on your designated computer.

Creating Simulated Web Content

1. Create a folder in the root directory of the C: drive named **Contoso**.

2. Create a folder in the root directory of the C: drive named **Docs**.

3. Inside the Docs folder, create a folder named **Project101**.

4. Open Notepad and type the following minimal HTML code:

```
<html>
<body>
<h1>Welcome to Contoso, Ltd.</h1>
<hr>
<p>Hello world and welcome to the new Contoso, Ltd., Web site!</p>
</body>
</html>
```

5. Save the file as "**C:\Contoso\Default.htm**," being certain to surround the name with quotation marks. Close Notepad.

6. Open Notepad and type the following minimal HTML code:

```
<html>
<body>
This is the site for Project 101
</body>
</html>
```

7. Save the file as "**C:\Docs\Project101\Default.htm**," being certain to surround the name with quotation marks. Close Notepad.

> **QUESTION**   Why should you select Default.htm as the name of the file rather than another name such as Pilot.htm or Testsite.htm?

Creating a New Web Site

1. Open the Internet Information Services (IIS) Manager snap-in from the Administrative Tools group.

2. In the scope pane, expand Web Sites\Default Web Site.

3. Right-click the Default Web Site and choose Stop.

4. Right-click the Web Sites node, point to New, and then choose Web Site.

    The Web Site Creation Wizard opens.

5. On the Web Site Description page, type the description **Contoso**. On the Web Site Home Directory page, set the path to **C:\Contoso**. All other default settings are acceptable. When you are finished, IIS Manager should look like Figure 7-2.

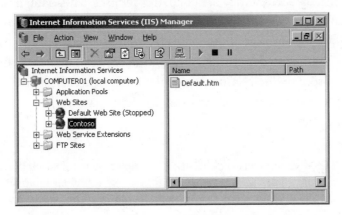

Figure 7-2   IIS Manager with the Contoso, Ltd., Web site

6. Test the Web site by opening Internet Explorer and entering **http://localhost** for the address. Internet Explorer should bring up a page that displays the text "Welcome to Contoso, Ltd." as shown in Figure 7-3.

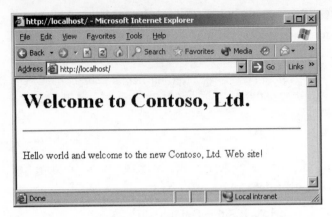

Figure 7-3   Default.htm for Contoso, Ltd., Web site

NOTE   You may receive messages regarding Internet Explorer Enhanced Security mode. If these messages appear, click OK to continue at each message.

EXERCISE 7-3: CREATING A SECURE VIRTUAL DIRECTORY

Estimated completion time: 10 minutes

The marketing department wants to have a secure Web site where sales representatives are able to access data when they are at client premises. This data, however, should not be able to be viewed by unauthorized users. As the IP addresses of the client sites will vary daily, access should be based on usernames and passwords assigned to the marketing department. To test that you can make this function and to train users from the marketing department in how to use such a site, you decide to create a secure virtual directory located off the main Web site. To do this, take the following steps:

IMPORTANT   If you have two computers, complete the following tasks on Computerxx. If you are working with a partner, you and your lab partner should separately complete the following tasks on your designated computer.

Creating a New Virtual Directory

1. In IIS Manager right-click the Contoso Ltd. site, point to New, and then choose Virtual Directory.

    The Virtual Directory Creation Wizard opens.

2. On the Virtual Directory Alias page, enter the alias **Project101**. On the Web Site Content Directory page, enter the path **C:\Docs\Project101**. Accept the other defaults.

   A new Project101 virtual directory appears in IIS Manager under the Contoso Ltd. Web site.

3. Test the Project101 virtual directory by opening Internet Explorer and entering **http://localhost/project101** for the address. Internet Explorer should bring up a page that displays the text "This is the site for Project 101."

   > **QUESTION** List several other URLs that you could use to display this same page.

Securing the Virtual Directory Content

1. In IIS Manager, open the Properties dialog box for the Project101 virtual directory.

2. Click the Directory Security tab.

3. In the Authentication And Access Control area, click Edit.

   The Authentication Methods dialog box opens.

4. Clear the Enable Anonymous Access check box as shown in Figure 7-4. Permission to the files in the site now requires valid user accounts.

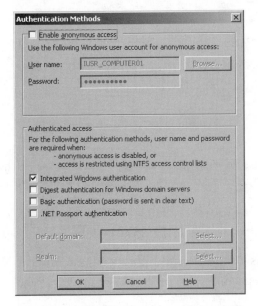

Figure 7-4 Disabling anonymous access

5. Click OK twice.

6. To check the security restriction, perform the following test:

If you are using Computer*xx*, open Internet Explorer and type **http://computerxx.contosoxx.com** for the address. If you are using Computer*yy*, open Internet Explorer and type **http://computeryy.contosoyy.contosoxx.com** for the address.

The Welcome To Contoso, Ltd., page should appear.

7. If you are using Computer*xx*, now type **http://computerxx.contosoxx.com/Project101** for the address. If you are using Computer*yy*, now type **http://computeryy.contosoyy.contosoxx.com/Project101** for the address.

The Connect To dialog box should appear and you are prompted for credentials to access the page as shown in Figure 7-5.

Figure 7-5   Connect To dialog box prompting for credentials to access page

8. Log on with the WEBUser account (specify the domain with the user name, such as contoso*xx*\webuser) and the Project101 homepage should appear.

> **QUESTION**   Even though you are logged in as Administrator and the Integrated Windows Authentication check box is selected in the Authentication Methods dialog box, why are you still prompted for credentials?

9. In Windows Explorer, open the Properties dialog box for C:\Docs\Project101\Default.htm and click the Security tab.

10. Change the NTFS permissions for the Default.htm document. Add the WEBUser account and set the permissions for WEBUser to Deny Read access.

11. When you close the Properties dialog box, click Yes in the Security dialog box that asks if you want to continue.

12. Close and reopen Internet Explorer. If you are using Computer*xx*, connect to **http://computerxx.contosoxx.com/Project101**. If you are using Computer*yy*, connect to **http://computeryy.contosoyy.contosoxx.com/Project101**.

13. The Connect To dialog box should appear.

14. Enter the credentials for WEBUser. If the Connect To dialog box reappears, enter credentials two more times.

   You should see a message that indicates you are not authorized to view this page, HTTP Error 401 Unauthorized, as shown in Figure 7-6.

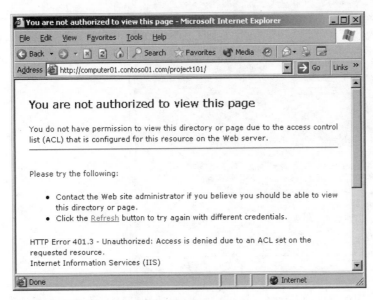

Figure 7-6 HTTP Error 401 Unauthorized

15. Close and reopen Internet Explorer. Connect to the same URL. When the Connect To dialog box appears, enter the credentials for Administrator. You should be able to view the page normally.

EXERCISE 7-4: SETTING UP AN FTP SERVER FOR ACCESS BY ONLY A SPECIFIC GROUP OF USERS

Estimated completion time: 10 minutes

You have been asked to set up an FTP site that can be accessed only by the FTPUsers group and administrator accounts. Users from Contoso, Ltd will access the site to upload and download files.

IMPORTANT   If you have two computers, complete the following tasks on Computerxx. If you are working with a partner, you and your lab partner should separately complete the following tasks on your designated computer.

1. Open IIS Manager and expand FTP Sites\Default FTP Site.

2. Open the Properties dialog box for the Default FTP Site.

3. On the Security Accounts tab, clear the Allow Anonymous Connections check box as shown in figure 7-7. When the warning message appears, click Yes.

4. In the Properties dialog box, click OK.

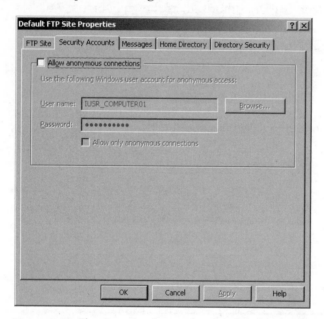

Figure 7-7   The Security Accounts tab of the Default FTP Site Properties

5. Using Windows Explorer, open the Properties dialog box for the C:\Inetpub\Ftproot folder.

6. On the Security tab, click Advanced.

   The Advanced Security Settings dialog box opens.

7. Clear the Allow Inheritable Permissions From The Parent check box.

8. In the Security dialog box that appears, click Copy.

9. Click OK in the Advanced Security Settings dialog box.

10. In the Properties dialog box, remove the Users group and add the FTPUsers group. Ensure that the FTPusers group has Read & Execute

(Allow), List Folder Contents (Allow), Read (Allow), and Write (Allow) permissions as shown Figure 7-8.

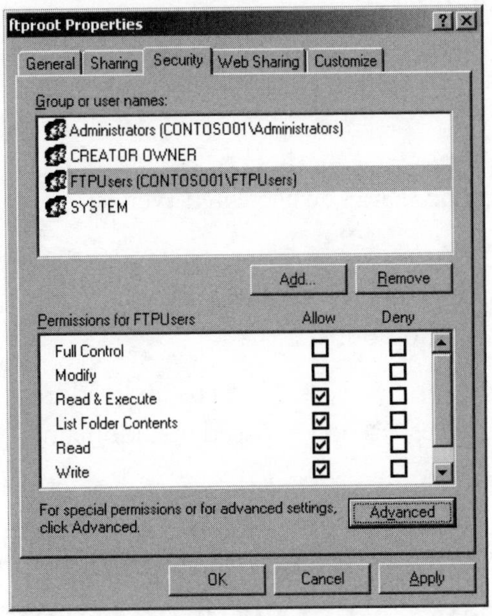

Figure 7-8   NTFS permissions on the Ftproot folder

11. Click OK in the Properties dialog box.

12. Open a command prompt.

13. Type the command **ftp localhost**

14. At the User prompt, type **WEBUser** and press Enter. At the Password prompt, type **P@ssw0rd** and press Enter.

    You will receive the message 530 User WEBUser cannot log in, home directory inaccessible. Login failed.

15. To exit the ftp prompt, type **bye** and press Enter.

16. Open Active Directory Users and Computers. Add the WEBUser account to the FTPUsers group.

17. Repeat steps 13 and 14. WEBUser should now have access to the FTP site. If you get the same error message, open the Services console in Administrative Tools, stop the FTP Publishing Service, and then restart it.

REVIEW QUESTIONS

Estimated completion time: 20 minutes

1. In your own words, describe what you learned during this lab.

2. Which files can be used for the default content page in the Default Web Site when IIS is first installed?

3. By default, to which application pool are newly created Web sites added?

4. The content for a site or virtual directory resource can come from three different locations. What are these locations?

5. Why is it easier for a computer to restrict access based on an IP address range than it is for a computer to restrict access based on a domain name?

LAB CHALLENGE 7-1: LOCKING DOWN IIS SO THAT IT CAN BE ACCESSED ONLY FROM A SPECIFIC IP ADDRESS

Estimated completion time: 10 minutes

You want to ensure that the entire Contoso, Ltd., Web site is visible from the computerxx.contosoxx.com, but you don't want the entire Web site to be accessible from the computeryy.contosoyy.contosoxx.com. Using the ability to restrict connections via IP address, how do you accomplish these goals?

IMPORTANT   *Complete the following tasks on Computerxx.*

LAB 8
SOFTWARE UPDATE SERVICES

Upon completion of this chapter, you will be able to:

- Exercise 8-1: Installing SUS

- Exercise 8-2: Synchronizing SUS and Approving Updates

- Exercise 8-3: Configuring Automatic Updates via Local Group Policy

- Lab Review Questions

- Lab Challenge 8-1: Configuring Automatic Updates via Active Directory

SCENARIO

One task that has consumed an inordinate amount of the Contoso, Ltd. systems administration department's time has been the management and deployment of patches. Before the company firewall was configured, Microsoft Windows 2000 and Microsoft Windows XP client systems would connect and download patches from the Windows Update servers. Whether or not these patches were installed was dependent on whether or not an administrator logged into the system and enabled them. As part of the move towards Microsoft Windows Server 2003, Contoso, Ltd. management would prefer a more centralized approach to the management of patches. A simple and effective method of doing this is to implement Software Update Services, a freely downloadable add-on to Windows Server 2003. As part of the Windows Server 2003 pilot program at Contoso, Ltd., you will set up a software update infrastructure using Software Update Services (SUS) as the cornerstone.

After completing this lab, you will be able to:

- Install SUS on a Windows Server 2003 computer

- Synchronize SUS with the Windows Update servers

- Prepare a list of approved patches to deploy across the organization

- Configure Group Policy to point to the organization's SUS server

Estimated lesson time: 85 minutes

BEFORE YOU BEGIN

To successfully complete this lab, you will need the following:

- A computer with Windows Server 2003 installed and configured as a domain controller. (See Lab Exercises 2-1 and 2-2.)

- The computer should have its own domain, which will either be named contoso*xx*.com or contoso*yy*.contoso*xx*.com.

- The Group Policy Management console installed. See Lab 3-1.

- Internet Information Services (IIS) installed. See Lab 7-1.

- Access to the SUS server installer, which is in the Lab Manual\Lab08 folder. Alternatively, you can download the SUS server installer from the following location: *http://go.microsoft.com/fwlink/?LinkId=6930.*

> **NOTE** This lab is written to be performed on two computers. If each student has only a single computer, students can work as partners and share computers when needed. The first computer will be Computer*xx* and the second computer will be Computer*yy*. Computer*xx* typically has an odd-numbered name, such as Computer01 and Computer03. Computer*yy* typically has an even-numbered name, such as Computer02 and Computer04. If you are unsure of your computers name, run a command prompt and issue the **hostname** command.

EXERCISE 8-1: INSTALLING SUS

Estimated completion time: 15 minutes

The first step in running your Software Update Services (SUS) pilot program is to install SUS. Because SUS requires IIS, and you have finished with the IIS pilot program, the Web server component of the domain controller can be re-tasked to host SUS.

IMPORTANT If you have two computers, complete the following tasks on Computerxx. If you are working with a partner, you and your lab partner should separately complete the following tasks on your designated computer.

To install SUS on the computer, perform the following tasks:

1. Log on to the computer as Administrator. Your username is **Administrator**. The password is P@ssw0rd. For Computerxx, select the contosoxx domain. For Computeryy, select the contosoyy domain.

2. Using the IIS Manager, stop the Default Web Site and stop the Contoso Web site created in Lab 7.

3. Disable Internet Explorer Enhanced Security Configuration for administrator groups. Open Add Or Remove Programs and then click Add/Remove Windows Components. In the Windows Components Wizard, select Internet Explorer Enhanced Security Configuration and then click Details. In the Internet Explorer Enhanced Security Configuration dialog box, clear the For Administrator Groups check box and click OK. Click Next and when the wizard finishes, click Finish.

4. Locate the SUS server installer in the Lab Manual\Lab08 folder, and start the SUS installation by double-clicking the file.

   The Microsoft Software Update Services Setup Wizard opens.

5. On the Welcome page, click Next.

6. On the End-User License Agreement page, read and accept the End User License Agreement and then click Next.

7. On the Choose Setup Type page, choose a Custom installation.

8. On the Choose File Locations page, choose the second option, Keep The Updates On A Microsoft Windows Update Server, as is shown in Figure 8-1. This saves you from having to download several hundred megabytes of files from the server. Click Next.

Figure 8-1   Specifying where to save updates

9. On the Handling New Versions Of Previously Approved Updates page, select the I Will Manually Approve New Versions Of Approved Updates option. Click Next.

10. On the Ready To Install page, the client download URL should be *http://computerxx* (or http://computeryy). Click Install.

11. When installation is complete, click Finish.

The SUS administration site (http://localhost/SUSAdmin/) should open in Internet Explorer automatically as shown in Figure 8-2.

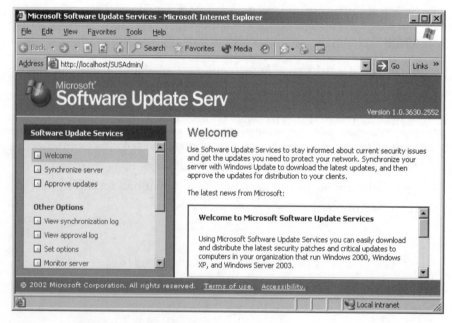

Figure 8-2   SUS administration site

12. In IIS Manager, refresh the Web Sites container.

QUESTION   What is different about the Web site's container in IIS Manager?

QUESTION   If you wanted other Web sites to be functional in addition to the SUS Web site, what action could you take?

EXERCISE 8-2: SYNCHRONIZING SUS AND APPROVING UPDATES

Estimated completion time: 15 minutes

Once SUS has been installed on the Windows Server 2003 domain controller, the most recent list of patches available from the servers at Microsoft is required. Because this list changes regularly, it must be downloaded from Microsoft (although it is possible to deploy a pre-downloaded list, this approach is not recommended). Downloading this list of patches and, optionally, downloading the patches themselves is known as synchronizing the server. Once the list of available patches is downloaded, the administrator is able to go through the list and approve those that are considered relevant to the organization.

IMPORTANT   If you have two computers, complete the following tasks on Computerxx. If you are working with a partner, you and your lab partner should separately complete the following tasks on your designated computer.

To synchronize the SUS server running on the Windows Server 2003 computer and view the list of updates that can be applied, perform the following steps:

NOTE   If you are not already viewing the SUS administration site, open Internet Explorer on your computer by navigating to *http://localhost/ SUSAdmin*.

1. In the left navigation pane, click Synchronize Server.

   The Synchronize Server page appears.

2. In the right pane, click Synchronization Schedule.

   The Schedule Synchronization dialog box opens as shown in Figure 8-3.

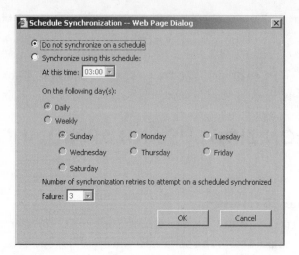

Figure 8-3   SUS Schedule Synchronization options

> **NOTE**   In this lab you will synchronize manually. However, you can examine synchronization options by clicking Synchronize Using This Schedule.

3. When you are finished exploring schedule synchronization options, click Cancel.

4. On the Synchronize Server page, click Synchronize Now. If your computer is not connected to the Internet, after a few moments a message will display indicating that the server was unable to synchronize. When you click OK it will display information from the synchronization log.

   SUS was installed with the option to keep the updates on the Microsoft Windows update server, however, if you have elected to download updates to the local server, synchronization would take several minutes depending on your Internet connection.

5. After synchronization has occurred, you will be redirected automatically to the Approve Updates page as shown in Figure 8-4. You can also click Approve Updates on the left navigation pane.

6. Examine other pages of the SUS administration site such as Set Options and Monitor Server. After you have familiarized yourself with the site, close Internet Explorer.

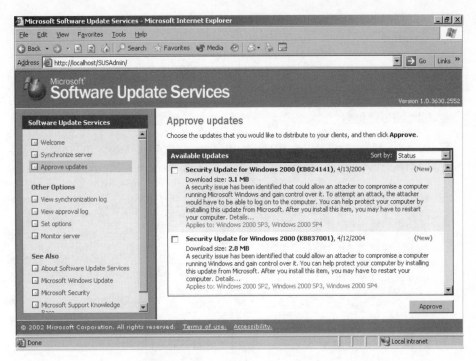

Figure 8-4   Updates awaiting approval

EXERCISE 8-3: CONFIGURING AUTOMATIC UPDATES VIA LOCAL GROUP POLICY

Estimated completion time: 15 minutes

As part of the SUS pilot program, you want to try SUS on a single Windows Server 2003 computer before deploying it via Group Policy to larger numbers of computers in the organization.

> **IMPORTANT**   If you have two computers, complete the following tasks on Computerxx. If you are working with a partner, you and your lab partner should separately complete the following tasks on your designated computer.

To configure a server via local Group Policy, perform the following steps:

1. In the Run dialog box, type **gpedit.msc**.

   The Group Policy Object Editor opens.

2. Navigate to Computer Configuration\Administrative Templates\Windows Components\Windows Update.

3. Double-click the policy Specify Intranet Microsoft Update Service Location.

The Specify Intranet Microsoft Update Service Location Properties dialog box opens.

4. Click Enabled.

5. In *both* text boxes, type http://computer*xx*.contoso*xx*.com (or http://computer*yy*.contoso*yy*.contoso*xx*.com) as shown in Figure 8-5.

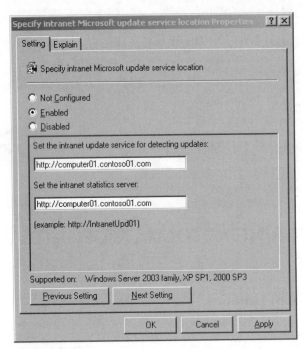

Figure 8-5   Specifying the SUS server where a computer should look for updates

6. Click OK.

7. Double-click the policy Configure Automatic Updates.

8. Click Enabled.

9. In the Configure Automatic Updating drop-down list, choose 4 – Auto Download And Schedule The Install.

> **QUESTION**   What are the other Configure Automatic Updating options and what is the benefit of selecting an option that does not notify for install?

10. Confirm the installation schedule as daily at 3:00 A.M. Click OK.

11. Double-click the policy Reschedule Automatic Updates Scheduled Installations.

12. Click Enabled.

13. In the Wait After System Startup (Minutes) box, type 1.

> **QUESTION**   What is the benefit of using the policy Reschedule Automatic Updates Scheduled Installations? Why would you do this?

14. Click OK in the Properties dialog box and close the Group Policy Object Editor.

REVIEW QUESTIONS

Estimated completion time: 20 minutes

1. In your own words, describe what you learned during this lab.

2. What are some of the benefits of storing update files locally on the SUS server?

3. What are some of the disadvantages of storing update files locally on the SUS server?

4. Why should updates deployed to client computers generally be configured to automatically install at a particular time?

5. What protocol is used to download the updates from the SUS server?

LAB CHALLENGE 8-1: CONFIGURING AUTOMATIC UPDATES VIA ACTIVE DIRECTORY

Estimated completion time: 20 minutes

The first stage of the SUS pilot program has been successful. Management has asked you to configure all of the computers located in the domain to use a SUS server for their updates. You want these computers to install any updates daily at 1:00 P.M. If the computer is not running at 1:00 P.M, any updates should be installed one minute after startup. Management would prefer you to use a new GPO rather than edit the default domain GPO.

What steps would you take to configure automatic updates? After automatic updates is configured, open the System control panel and click the Automatic Updates tab. Are there any changes on the Automatic Updates tab? Take a screen shot of this tab.

TROUBLESHOOTING LAB B

TROUBLESHOOTING IIS AND REMOTE DESKTOP FOR ADMINISTRATION

Troubleshooting Lab B is a practical application of the knowledge you have acquired from Labs 5 through 8. Your instructor or lab assistant has changed your computer configuration, causing it to "break." Your task in this lab will be to apply your acquired skills to troubleshoot and resolve the break. A scenario will be presented which will lay out the parameters of the break and the conditions that must be met for the scenario to be resolved. This troubleshooting lab has two break scenarios. The first break scenario involves IIS (Internet Information Services) permissions and the second break scenario involves Remote Desktop for Administration.

> **NOTE Do not proceed with this lab until you receive guidance from your instructor.** The break scenario that you will be performing will depend on which computer you are using. The first computer will be Computerxx and the second computer will be Computeryy. Computerxx typically has an odd-numbered name, such as Computer01 and Computer03. Computeryy typically has an even numbered name, such as Computer02 and Computer04 . If you are unsure of your computers name, run a command prompt and issue the **hostname** command. If you are using Computerxx, you will perform Break Scenario 1. If you are using Computeryy, you will perform Break Scenario 2. Your instructor or lab assistant may also have special instructions. Consult with your instructor before proceeding.

Break Scenario 1

> **IMPORTANT** Perform this break scenario on Computerxx.

Contoso, Ltd. is a large accounting firm with offices in twenty cities. The company network contains five member servers running Windows Server 2003, Standard Edition, 200 client computers running Windows XP Professional, and three domain controllers running Windows Server 2003, Enterprise Edition. All computers are configured in a single Active Directory site.

One of the Windows Server 2003 systems is running IIS and hosts the company's public Web site and a virtual directory related to Project101—a project on which Contoso, Ltd. and its customer are collaborating. Security policy specifies that the company's Web site (*http://computerxx.contosoxx.com*) should be accessible to the general public without requiring authentication; and that project-specific virtual directories (*http://computerxx.contosoxx.com/project101/*) should only be accessible to authenticated users who are working on that project.

You are part of a team of network consultants that is helping Contoso, Ltd. maintain its Windows servers. As the project comes to a close, you are tasked with ensuring that security policies are, in fact, being followed and that the implementation is correct.

The user account WEBUser represents one of the individuals involved with Project101. The password for WEBUser is P@ssw0rd. Be sure to test the company Web site and the Project101 virtual directory to identify any behaviors that do not comply with company security policy.

As you resolve the problem, fill out the worksheet in the TroubleshootingLabB folder and include the following information:

- Description of the problem.

- A list of all steps taken to diagnose the problem, even the ones that did not work.

- Description of the exact issue and solution.

- A list of the tools and resources you used to help solve this problem.

Break Scenario 2

IMPORTANT *Perform this break scenario on Computeryy.*

Contoso, Ltd. is a large accounting firm with offices in twenty cities. The company network contains five member servers running Windows Server 2003, Standard Edition, 200 client computers running Windows XP Professional, and three domain controllers running Windows Server 2003, Enterprise Edition. All computers are configured in a single Active Directory domain.

Administrators at Contoso, Ltd. manage servers using Remote Desktop for Administration. You are a network engineer and receive a telephone call from an administrator who is unable to remotely administer one of the servers, Computeryy. Access to other servers continues to function as expected using the same user account.

You are currently sitting in front of Computeryy. Simulate the administrator's problem by using Remote Desktop Connection to attempt to connect to Computeryy using the localhost computer name. Troubleshoot Computeryy and determine why the administrator is unable to connect via Remote Desktop for Administration using the Administrator account.

As you resolve the problem, fill out the worksheet in the TroubleshootingLabB folder and include the following information:

- Description of the problem.

- A list of all steps taken to diagnose the problem, even the ones that did not work.

- Description of the exact issue and solution.

- A list of the tools and resources you used to help solve this problem.

DNS INSTALLATION AND CONFIGURATION

Upon completion of this chapter, you will be able to:

■ Exercise 9-1: Installing and Testing a DNS Server

■ Exercise 9-2: Configuring Active Directory Integrated and Standard Primary Zones

■ Exercise 9-3: Configuring a Secondary Zone

■ Lab Review Questions

■ Lab Challenge 9-1: Creating Resource Records

SCENARIO

The rollout of Microsoft Windows Server 2003 at Contoso, Ltd. will involve the extensive use of DNS. Until this point Contoso, Ltd. relied upon WINS for internal name resolution. With the move to Windows Server 2003, the implementation of DNS becomes important. Prior to this Contoso Ltd.'s ISP was used for external DNS resolution and internal DNS resolution was not necessary.

After completing this lab, you will be able to:

■ Install the DNS service on Windows Server 2003

■ Configure a primary DNS zones

■ Configure a secondary DNS zone

Estimated lesson time: 90 minutes

BEFORE YOU BEGIN

To successfully complete this lab, you will need to have completed the following labs:

- A computer with Windows Server 2003 installed and configured as a domain controller. (See Lab Exercises 2-1 and 2-2.)

- The computer should have its own domain, which will either be contoso*xx*.com or contoso*yy*.contoso*xx*.com.

> **NOTE** This lab is written to be performed on two computers. If each student has only a single computer, students can work as partners and share computers when needed. The first computer will be Computerxx and the second computer will be Computeryy. Computerxx typically has an odd-numbered name, such as Computer01 and Computer03. Computeryy typically has an even-numbered name, such as Computer02 and Computer04. If you are unsure of your computers name, run a command prompt and issue the **hostname** command.

EXERCISE 9-1: INSTALLING AND TESTING A DNS SERVER

Estimated completion time: 20 minutes

The first step that you need to take in implementing a DNS name resolution structure for Contoso, Ltd. is to install the DNS server. Because you want to explore the functionality of DNS, and you know that there is already a DNS server installed on the domain controller for the parent domain (which was configured during the setup of the Active Directory directory service), you have decided to install DNS on the domain controller in the child domain.

> **IMPORTANT** Complete the following tasks on Computeryy.

1. Log on to Computeryy as **Administrator**. The password is P@ssw0rd. Select the contosoyy domain.

2. Open Control Panel and then click Add Or Remove Programs.

3. Click Add/Remove Windows Components.

   The Windows Components Wizard opens.

4. In the Components area, highlight the Networking Services component. Be sure not to select the Networking Services check box. Click Details.

The Networking Services dialog box opens.

5. In the Subcomponents Of Networking Services area, select the Domain Name System (DNS) check box as shown in Figure 9-1.

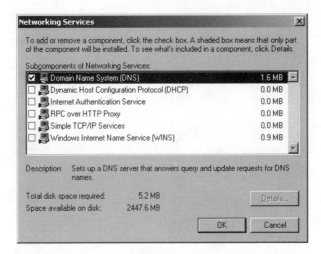

Figure 9-1   Selecting the DNS component in the Networking Services area of Add/Remove Windows components.

6. Click OK, and then click Next. You might be asked to insert the Windows Server 2003 CD.

7. When the installation completes, click Finish.

8. Close the Add Or Remove Programs window.

9. Open the DNS console from the Administrative Tools menu.

10. In the scope pane, select Computeryy.

11. Right-click Computeryy and select Properties.

12. In the Properties dialog box, click the Monitoring tab.

13. Select the A Simple Query Against This DNS Server check box and then click Test Now. The result of this test will be displayed in the Test Results area, shown in Figure 9-2.

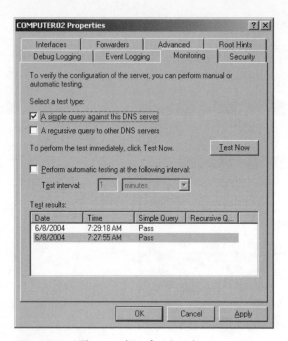

Figure 9-2   The results of a simple query test against the newly installed DNS server.

14. Click OK to close the Properties dialog box and then close the DNS console.

EXERCISE 9-2: CONFIGURING ACTIVE DIRECTORY INTEGRATED AND STANDARD PRIMARY ZONES

Estimated completion time: 20 minutes

Part of the task of creating a DNS infrastructure for Contoso, Ltd. is the deployment of primary zones. Although a primary zone exists on the domain controller, you wish to experiment with other primary zone configurations on the Windows Server 2003 pilot network.

> **IMPORTANT**   The following tasks must be completed on both Computerxx and Computeryy, with the relevant computer indicated at each time.

To create these primary zones, take the following steps:

1. Log on to the computer as **Administrator**. The password is P@ssw0rd. For Computerxx, select the contosoxx domain. For Computeryy, select the contosoyy domain.

2. Open the DNS console.

3. On Computerxx only, expand the Forward Lookup Zones node. Right-click the contosoxx.com node and select Properties. On the General tab, click Change next to the Replication setting to open the Change Zone Replication Scope dialog box. Select the To All DNS Servers In The Active Directory Forest option and click OK. Click OK to close the Properties dialog box.

4. In the scope pane, select the computer.

5. Right-click the computer and select New Zone.

   The New Zone Wizard opens.

6. On the Zone Type page select Primary Zone. Ensure that the Store The Zone In Active Directory check box is selected. Click Next.

7. On the Active Directory Zone Replication Scope page, select the first option To All DNS Servers In The Active Directory Forest. Click Next.

8. On the Forward Or Reverse Lookup Zone page, select Forward Lookup Zone. Click Next.

9. On the Zone Name page type the zone name. If you are using Computerxx, set the zone name to **wingtiptoysxx.com**. If you are using Computeryy, set the zone name to **tailspintoysyy.com**. Click Next.

10. On the Dynamic Update page, ensure Allow Only Secure Dynamic Updates is selected. Click Next.

11. On the final page, click Finish.

    A dialog box might appear indicating that the zone cannot be replicated to all DNS servers in the forest because the required application directory partition does not exist. If this dialog box appears, click OK.

12. In the DNS console, expand Forward Lookup Zones. The new zone that you configured should be visible.

13. On Computerxx, open the Active Directory Sites and Services console and select the Sites\Default-First-Site-Name\Servers\Computerxx\NTDS Settings node. In the details pane, right-click the connection and select Replicate Now. Click OK to the message informing you that Active Directory connection replication has occurred.

14. Return to the DNS console and refresh. The new zone created on the partner computer should now appear in the DNS console as shown in Figure 9-3.

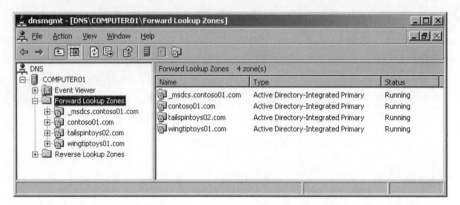

Figure 9-3 Zones configured on the partner computer appear after Active Directory replication occurs.

> **QUESTION** What would have happened if you hadn't forced replication on Computerxx?

15. In the DNS console, right-click the Forward Lookup Zones node and select New Zone. This starts the New Zone Wizard again. Click Next.

16. On the Zone Type page, select Primary Zone and clear the Store The Zone In Active Directory check box. Click Next.

17. On the Zone Name page, type the zone name. On Computerxx, set the new zone name to **prosewarexx.com**. On Computeryy, set the new zone name to **litwareincyy.com**. Click Next.

18. On the Zone File page, leave the default new zone file name and click Next.

19. On the Dynamic Updates page, leave the default Do Not Allow Dynamic Updates. Click Next. Click Finish.

    The new zone appears in Forward Lookup Zones.

EXERCISE 9-3: CONFIGURING A SECONDARY ZONE

Estimated completion time: 15 minutes

Once you have established that you are able to create and manipulate primary zones in the Contoso, Ltd. pilot environment, the next step is to configure a secondary zone. A secondary zone can be used to replicate the data in the primary zone. As part of the Windows Server 2003 pilot program at Contoso Ltd., you will replicate primary zone data stored on the parent domain controller to the child domain controller.

To configure the secondary zone, take the following steps:

IMPORTANT   *Complete the following tasks on Computerxx.*

1. On Computerxx, open the DNS console.

2. Select the prosewarexx.com zone.

3. Right-click the prosewarexx.com zone and select Properties.

4. Click the Zone Transfers tab. Ensure that the Allow Zone Transfers check box is selected and that the Only To Servers Listed On The Name Servers Tab option is selected, as shown in Figure 9-4.

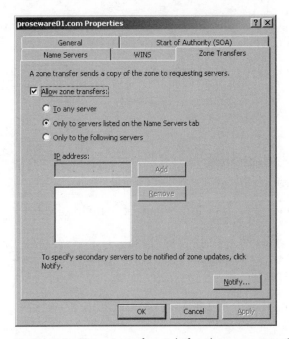

Figure 9-4   Zone transfers tab for the proseware01.com zone.

5. Click the Name Servers tab and click the Add button.

   The New Resource Record dialog box opens.

6. Enter the Server Fully Qualified Domain Name for Computeryy (**computeryy.contosoyy.contosoxx.com**).

7. Click Resolve. The IP address of Computeryy should appear in the list. Click OK.

8. Click OK again to close the prosewarexx.com zone Properties dialog box.

IMPORTANT   *Complete the following tasks on Computeryy.*

9. On Computeryy, open the DNS console.

10. Select the Forward Lookup Zones node.

11. Right-click the Forward Lookup Zones node and select New Zone.

    The New Zone Wizard opens.

12. On the Zone Type page, select Secondary Zone. Click Next.

13. On the Zone Name page, type **prosewarexx.com**. Click Next.

14. On the Master DNS Servers page, enter the IP address of Computerxx
    and then click Add. Click Next.

15. On the final page, click Finish.

    The secondary zone should appear in Forward Lookup Zones.

REVIEW QUESTIONS

Estimated completion time: 20 minutes

1. In your own words, describe what you learned during this lab.

2. In what cases does an Active Directory-Integrated Zone not replicate to
    all DNS servers in a forest?

3. Which zone was not present on Computerxx, but was present on Com-
    puteryy at the end of the lab?

4. Why would you want to restrict zone transfers to only those servers on
    the Name Servers tab?

5. Why did the Store The Zone In Active Directory check box become
    grayed out when you created a secondary zone on Computeryy, even
    though Computeryy is a domain controller?

LAB CHALLENGE 9-1: CREATING RESOURCE RECORDS

Estimated completion time: 15 minutes

Because you will not be instituting dynamic updates on some of the zones at
Contoso Ltd., DNS resource records will need to be created manually. To practice
this process, use the DNS console to create the following records:

On Computerxx, create the following records:

- testhost.tailspintoysyy.com   10.1.1.200

- host-one.wingtiptoysxx.com   10.1.1.201

- another-host.contosoxx.com   10.1.1.202

- fileserver.contosoyy.contosoxx.com   10.1.1.203

On Computeryy, create the following records:

- host-three.contosoxx.com   10.1.1.204

- printserver.contosoyy.contosoxx.com   10.1.1.205

- books.litwareincyy.com   10.1.1.206

After you have created the records, force a replication and check that the records appear in the DNS console of your partner's computer.

LAB 10
ADVANCED DNS CONCEPTS

Upon completion of this chapter, you will be able to:

- Exercise 10-1: Creating a Zone to be Delegated

- Exercise 10-2: Adding Host (A) Resource Records to the New Zone

- Exercise 10-3: Creating a Delegation

- Exercise 10-4: Creating a Stub Zone

- Lab Review Questions

- Lab Challenge 10-1: Configuring a Reverse Lookup Zone

SCENARIO

The DNS pilot program at Contoso, Ltd. is entering its final phases. You have been instructed to evaluate in the Contoso, Ltd. environment whether utilizing several advanced DNS concepts such as zone delegation and the use of stub zones would be appropriate. To do this, continue to use the Microsoft Windows Server 2003 domain controller and member server with which you completed the first rounds of the DNS pilot program.

After completing this lab, you will be able to:

- Add hosts to a zone using the DNS console

- Create a zone delegation

- Create a stub zone

Estimated lesson time: 100 minutes

BEFORE YOU BEGIN

To successfully complete this lab, you will need to have completed the following labs:

- A computer with Windows Server 2003 installed and configured as a domain controller. (See Lab Exercises 2-1 and 2-2.)

- The computer should have its own domain, which will either be be named contosoxx.com or contosoyy.contosoxx.com.

- The domain functional level must be set to Windows 2000 native or Windows Server 2003. (See Lab Challenge 2-1).

- Have set up several primary DNS zones. (See Lab Exercises 9-1, 9-2, and 9-3)

> **NOTE**   This lab is written to be performed on two computers. If each student has only a single computer, students can work as partners and share computers when needed. The first computer will be Computerxx and the second computer will be Computeryy. Computerxx typically has an odd-numbered name, such as Computer01 and Computer03. Computeryy typically has an even-numbered name, such as Computer02 and Computer04. If you are unsure of your computers name, run a command prompt and issue the **hostname** command.

EXERCISE 10-1: CREATING A ZONE TO BE DELEGATED

Estimated completion time: 10 minutes

The first step in exploring the concept of delegation is creating a test zone to be delegated. For a delegation to succeed from one DNS server to a second DNS server, the delegated zone must exist on the second server.

> **IMPORTANT**   The following tasks must be completed on both Computerxx and Computeryy. Some steps have computer specific instructions.

To create the zone that will be delegated, perform the following steps:

1. Log on to the computer as **Administrator**. The password is P@ssw0rd. For Computerxx, select the contosoxx domain. For Computeryy, select the contosoyy domain.

2. Open the DNS console.

3. In the DNS console tree, expand the computer node, right-click the Forward Lookup Zones node, and select New Zone.

   The New Zone Wizard opens.

4. If you are using Computer*xx*, create a new Primary Zone named **sub.litwareincyy.com.** If you are using Computer*yy*, create a new Primary Zone named **sub.prosewarexx.com.** Use the default settings in the wizard for zone creation.

EXERCISE 10-2: ADDING HOST (A) RESOURCE RECORDS TO THE NEW ZONE

Estimated completion time: 15 minutes

To be tested, the delegated subdomain must contain some host records. Because there are no appropriate hosts on the pilot network at present, you need to create host records in the new subdomain. The creation of these records will not interfere with the pre-existing records.

> **IMPORTANT**   The following tasks must be completed on both Computer*xx* and Computer*yy*. Some steps have computer specific instructions.

To create these new records, perform the following steps:

1. Open the DNS console.

2. Expand to the Forward Lookup Zones node.

3. If you are using Computer*xx*, select the sub.litwareincyy.com node. If you are using Computer*yy*, select the sub.prosewarexx.com node.

4. Right-click the selected node and select New Host (A).

   The New Host dialog box appears.

5. If you are using Computer*xx*, in the Name text box, type **Server***yy* and enter the IP address of Computer*yy*. If you are using Computer*yy*, in the Name text box, type **Server***xx* and enter the IP address of Computer*xx*. Do not create an associated pointer (PTR) record.

6. Click Add Host.

7. In the message box that indicates that the host record was successfully created, click OK.

8. Click Done to close the New Host dialog box.

EXERCISE 10-3: CREATING A DELEGATION

Estimated completion time: 15 minutes

Once the preparations have been made, it is possible to create a delegation from the parent zone to the child zone. Delegations are important because DNS works hierarchically. Any request from outside the zone for a resource record in the delegated zone will have to pass through the DNS server that hosts the parent zone.

> **IMPORTANT**   The following tasks must be completed on both Computerxx and Computeryy. Some steps have computer specific instructions.

To configure the server that hosts the parent zone to process correctly a query on a host in the child zone, perform the following steps:

1. If you are using Computerxx, expand Forward Lookup Zones, and select the prosewarexx.com node. If you are using Computeryy, expand Forward Lookup Zones, and select the litwareincyy.com node.

2. Right-click the node and select New Delegation.

   The New Delegation Wizard opens.

3. On the Delegated Domain Name page, in the Delegated Domain text box, type **sub** and then click Next.

4. On the Name Servers page, click Add.

   The New Resource Record dialog box opens.

5. If you are using Computerxx, type **computeryy.contosoyy.contosoxx.com** in the Server Fully Qualified Domain Name box. If you are using Computeryy, type **computerxx.contosoxx.com** in the Server Fully Qualified Domain Name box.

6. Click Resolve.

   The IP address should appear in the list.

7. Click OK to close the New Resource Record dialog box.

8. Click Next and then click Finish.

9. Test that the delegation has worked. On Computerxx, open a command prompt and enter the command **nslookup serverxx.sub.prosewarexx.com**. On Computeryy, open a command prompt and enter the command **nslookup serverxx.sub.litwareincyy.com**.

10. Although the server name can't be found, both should return the same IP address.

> **QUESTION**   What IP address is returned after you perform both of these nslookup commands?

EXERCISE 10-4: CREATING A STUB ZONE

Estimated completion time: 20 minutes

Zone delegations require that the server hosting the parent zone keep an accurate record of the name servers hosting the child zone. With a standard delegation there is no way for the server hosting the child zone to automatically update the server hosting the parent zone if the name servers hosting the child zone are changed. A solution to this problem is to use stub zones, which regularly transfer a list of authoritative name servers from the child zone. Because Contoso, Ltd. will have diverse branches that might not keep head office informed if they move the server hosting their child DNS zone, the use of stub zones ensures that connectivity and referrals can continue with little need for administrator oversight.

> **IMPORTANT**   The following tasks must be completed on both Computerxx and Computeryy. Some steps have computer-specific instructions.

To create a stub zone, perform the following steps:

1. Open the DNS console.

2. On Computerxx, expand Forward Lookup Zones, and select sub.litwareincyy.com. On Computeryy, expand Forward Lookup Zones, and select sub.prosewarexx.com.

3. Right-click the selected node and select Properties.

   The Properties dialog box opens.

4. Click the Zone Transfers tab.

5. Select the Allow Zone Transfers check box and select the Only To Servers Listed On The Name Servers Tab option.

6. Click the Name Servers tab.

7. Click Add.

   The New Resource Record dialog box opens.

8. If you are using Computerxx, type **computeryy.contosoyy.contosoxx.com** in the Server Fully Qualified Domain Name box. If you are using Computeryy, type **computerxx.contosoxx.com** in the Server Fully Qualified Domain Name box.

9. Click Resolve.

   The IP address should appear in the list.

10. Click OK to close the New Resource Record dialog box.

11. Click OK to close the Properties dialog box.

> **QUESTION** Why must you enable zone transfers from the child domain to the parent domain when configuring a stub zone on the parent server?

12. Select the Forward Lookup Zones node.

13. Right-click the Forward Lookup Zones node and select New Zone.

    The New Zone Wizard opens.

14. On the Zone Type page select Stub Zone. Leave the Store The Zone In Active Directory check box selected. Click Next.

15. On the Active Directory Zone Replication Scope page, leave the To All DNS Servers In The Active Directory Domain option selected. Click Next.

16. On the Zone Name page, type the zone name. On Computerxx, type the zone name **sub.prosewarexx.com**. On Computeryy, type the zone name **sub.litwareincyy.com**. Click Next.

17. On the Master DNS Servers page, add the IP address of the DNS servers from which you want to copy the zone. On Computerxx, add the IP address of Computeryy to the Master DNS Servers list. On Computeryy, add the IP address of Computerxx to the Master DNS Servers list. Click Next.

18. Click Finish.

> **QUESTION** Compare the records located in the sub.prosewarexx.com zone on Computerxx to the sub.prosewarexx.com zone on Computeryy. What, if anything, are the differences?

REVIEW QUESTIONS

Estimated completion time: 20 minutes

1. In your own words, describe what you learned during this lab.

2. What are some common reasons for creating a zone delegation?

3. Before you delegate a zone from the server hosting the primary zone, what steps must you take on the server that will be hosting the delegated zone?

4. Why is it good administrative practice to create a stub zone for a zone that has been delegated from a DNS server?

5. Provide a list of all of the Forward Lookup Zones and type of zone for Computerxx after you've finished Lab 9 and Lab 10.

LAB CHALLENGE 10-1: CONFIGURING A REVERSE LOOKUP ZONE

Estimated completion time: 20 minutes

Reverse lookup zones host the resource records that reverse queries use to resolve IP addresses into fully qualified domain names (FQDN). Configure Computerxx to host an Active Directory-integrated reverse lookup zone, replicated to all domain controllers within the forest, for the IP subnet 192.168.10.0, 255.255.255.0. Configure Computeryy to host an Active Directory integrated reverse lookup zone, replicated to all domain controllers within the forest, for the IP subnet 192.168.20.0, 255.255.255.0. The zone should allow secure dynamic updates only.

When finished, take a screenshot of the expanded Reverse Lookup Zones node in the DNS console as well as the General tab of the new zone's properties.

LAB 11
WINDOWS SERVER SECURITY

Upon completion of this chapter, you will be able to:

- Exercise 11-1: Creating a Securable Structure for Servers

- Exercise 11-2: Creating and Configuring Security Templates for the Domain Controller

- Exercise 11-3: Using the Templates to Create and Apply Security Settings Through Group Policies

- Exercise 11-4: Modeling Resultant Set of Policy Using the Group Policy Management Console

- Lab Review Questions

- Lab Challenge 11-1: Creating More Templates and Policies

- Post-Lab Cleanup

SCENARIO

You are a domain administrator for Contoso, Ltd. Contoso, Ltd. has a large multi-domain Active Directory network with contoso*xx*.com as its root domain. You are responsible for the creation and deployment of security GPOs that conform to the Microsoft Solutions for Security outlined in documentation published in the Microsoft Windows Server 2003 Security Guide, *http://go.microsoft.com/fwlink/ ?linkid=14845*.

Your responsibility will be to configure hardened domain controllers, hardened file servers, hardened Web servers, and hardened infrastructure servers using guidelines and strategies outlined in the security guide. When you follow the objectives in this lab, you will:

- Design the appropriate inter-relationship and the appropriate level to link GPOs: site, domain, parent or child OU.

- Configure GPOs based on a suggested list of Group Policy settings.

- Configure Block Inheritance and No Override GPO options as appropriate.

After completing this lab, you will be able to:

- Design a multi-server domain security architecture.
- Create custom templates.
- Import templates into Group Policies.
- Deploy and combine multiple Group Policies.
- Configure GPO options.
- Disable Computer Configuration or User Configuration policies.

Estimated lesson time: 125 minutes

BEFORE YOU BEGIN

To successfully complete this lab, you will need the following:

- A computer with Windows Server 2003 installed and configured as a domain controller. (See Lab Exercises 2-1 and 2-2.)

- The computer should have its own domain, which will either be named contoso*xx*.com or contoso*yy*.contoso*xx*.com.

- The domain functional level must be set to Windows 2000 native or Windows Server 2003. (See Lab Challenge 2-1).

- Have installed the Group Policy Management console. (See Lab Exercise 3-1)

> **NOTE**   This lab is written to be performed on two computers. If each student has only a single computer, students can work as partners and share computers when needed. The first computer will be Computer*xx* and the second computer will be Computer*yy*. Computer*xx* typically has an odd-numbered name, such as Computer01 and Computer03. Computer*yy* typically has an even numbered name, such as Computer02 and Computer04. If you are unsure of your computers name, run a command prompt and issue the **hostname** command.

EXERCISE 11-1: CREATING A SECURABLE STRUCTURE FOR SERVERS

Estimated completion time: 10 minutes

The Contoso domain is comprised of multiple servers. Some are dedicated file servers, others are dedicated Web servers, and some are infrastructure servers responsible for DHCP address distribution and WINS name resolution. To manage these diverse servers, the contoso*xx*.com domain is designed with an "umbrella" organizational unit named Member Servers that contains multiple sub-organizational units designed to segregate security settings for various server roles. The parent OU, named Member Servers, contains three sub-organizational unites named File Servers, Web Servers, and Infrastructure Servers. The File Servers OU contains the computer objects configured as file servers. The Web Servers OU contains computer objects configured as Web servers, and the Infrastructure Servers OU contains computers running Windows Server 2003 hosting the WINS and DHCP services.

> **IMPORTANT**   If you have two computers, complete the following tasks on Computerxx. If you are working with a partner, you and your lab partner should separately complete the following tasks on your designated computer. Some steps have computer specific instructions.

Installing DHCP and WINS

To install DHCP and WINS, follow these steps:

1. Log on to the computer as Administrator. The password is **P@ssw0rd**. For Computer*xx*, select the contoso*xx* domain. For Computer*yy*, select the contoso*yy* domain.

2. Open the Add Or Remove Programs control panel and click Add/ Remove Windows Components.

   The Windows Component Wizard opens.

3. In the list of components, select Networking Services and click Details.

   The Networking Services dialog box opens.

4. Add check marks next to Dynamic Host Configuration Protocol (DHCP) and Windows Internet Name Service (WINS) and then click OK.

5. Click Next to install the components. You might be asked to insert your Windows Server 2003 CD.

6. When installation completes, click Finish.

Creating a Server Structure

To create a secure server structure, follow these steps:

1. Open the Active Directory Users and Computers console.

2. In the contosoxx.com (or contosoyy.contosoxx.com if you are using Computeryy) container, create a new organizational unit named Member Servers. (See Lab 3 if you need more detailed instructions.)

3. Create a sub-organizational unit within Member Servers named Web Servers.

4. Repeat the previous step to create two more organizational units within Member Servers named File Servers and Infrastructure Servers.

> **QUESTION**   What advantages are there to laying out the organizational units in this fashion?

EXERCISE 11-2: CREATING AND CONFIGURING SECURITY TEMPLATES FOR THE DOMAIN CONTROLLER

Estimated completion time: 35 minutes

You now need to create new individual security templates for the domain and configure their settings based on industry prescribed guidelines. In this exercise, you will create separate security templates that will ultimately be used to build group policies which will apply to the appropriate objects within the Active Directory.

> **IMPORTANT**   If you have two computers, complete the following tasks on Computerxx. If you are working with a partner, you and your lab partner should separately complete the following tasks on your designated computer. Some steps have computer specific instructions.

Creating a Security Templates Console

The first step is to create a Security Templates console. You will use this customized console to construct the necessary security templates.

1. Open up a blank Microsoft Management Console by choosing Start, Run, typing **mmc** and pressing ENTER.

   An empty console window opens.

2. In the empty console, choose File, Add/Remove Snap-in.

   The Add/Remove Snap-in dialog box opens.

3. Click Add.

   The Add Standalone Snap-in dialog box opens.

4. In the Available Standalone Snap-in list, select Security Templates, click Add, and then click Close.

5. Click OK to close the Add/Remove Snap-in dialog box.

   The Security Templates snap-in should now be added to the console root.

6. Save the console by clicking File and then Save.

   The Save As dialog box opens.

7. Save the console as **My Security Template Console**.

   To open the My Security Template Console after if has been closed, start MMC and open it using the File menu or click Start, All Programs, Administrative Tools, My Security Template Console.

Creating and Configuring the Domain Level Security Template

Once My Security Template Console has been created, the next step is to create the first customized security template that will be linked to the domain. Follow these steps:

1. In the scope pane of My Security Template Console, expand Security Templates to reveal the default folder location to the Microsoft built-in security templates.

2. Right-click the default folder location, and select New Template.

   The templates dialog box opens.

3. Enter the template name **Domain Level Security Template** and enter the description **Applied to Domain, elevates Password and Logon security**. Click OK.

In the list of security templates, you should see the Domain Level Security Template you've just created. Once the template is created you must customize the settings that will ultimately be propagated to all the computers and users in the domain.

4. Double-click the Domain Level Security Template to reveal the seven different sub-containers of settings that it contains, as shown in Figure 11-1.

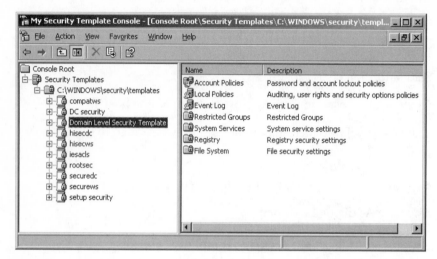

Figure 11-1   The seven sub-containers of the new Domain Level Security Template.

5. List the policies settings in the Domain Level Security Template\Account Policies\Password Policy container.

6. Customize the following settings:

   ❏ Enforce password history – 24 passwords remembered

   ❏ Maximum password age – 42 days (The value for the Maximum Password Age setting can be configured to never expire by setting the number of days to 0.)

   ❏ Minimum password age – 2 days

   ❏ Minimum password Length – 8 characters

   ❏ Password must meet complexity requirements – Enabled

   ❏ The password is at least six characters long. The password contains characters from three of the following four categories:

      – The password is at least six characters long. The password contains characters from three of the following four categories:

- English uppercase characters (A – Z)

- English lowercase characters (a – z)

- Base 10 digits (0 – 9)

- Non-alphanumeric (For example: !, $, #, or %)

- The password does not contain three or more characters from the user's account name.

- This setting combined with a Minimum Password Length of 8, ensures that there are at least 218,340,105,584,896 different possibilities for a single password.

❑ Store Passwords Using Reversible Encryption - Disabled

7. In the Account Lockout Policy container, configure the following:

❑ Account lockout duration – 20 minutes

❑ Account lockout threshold – 50 invalid logon attempts

❑ Reset account lockout counter after – 20 minutes

QUESTION   What is the purpose of the 50 invalid logon attempts setting?

NOTE   Account policies are implemented at the domain level. A Microsoft Windows Server 2003 domain must have a single password policy, account lockout policy, and Kerberos version 5 authentication protocol policy for the domain. Setting these policies at any other level in Active Directory will only affect local accounts on member servers. If there are groups that require separate password policies, they should be segmented into another domain or forest based on any additional requirements.

By default, workstations and servers joined to a domain, and the domain member computers, also receive the same account policy for their local accounts. However, local account policies for member computers can be differentiated from the domain account policy by defining an account policy for the OU that contains the member computers. The Account Policies settings can be configured in the following location within the Group Policy Object Editor: Computer Configuration\Windows Settings\Security Settings\Account Policies\Password Policy.

Creating and Configuring the Member Server Baseline Security Template

In this section, you will create another security template named Member Server Baseline. Follow these steps:

1. In the My Security Template Console, create a new template named **Member Server Baseline**.

2. Expand the Member Server Baseline\Local Policies container.

3. In the Audit Policy container, configure the following settings:

   ❑ Audit account logon events – Success, Failure

   ❑ Audit account management – Success, Failure

   ❑ Audit directory Service access – Success, Failure

   ❑ Audit logon events – Success, Failure

   ❑ Audit object access – Success, Failure

   ❑ Audit policy change – Success

   ❑ Audit privilege use – Failure

   ❑ Audit process tracking – No Auditing

   ❑ Audit system events – Success

4. In the User Rights Assignment container, configure the following settings:

   ❑ Allow log on locally – Administrators, Backup Operators, Server Operators

   ❑ Allow log on through Terminal Services – Administrators, Remote Desktop Users

   ❑ Deny access to this computer from the network – ANONYMOUS LOGON, Built-in Administrator, Guests, Support_388945a0.

   NOTE Support_388945a0 is a default member of the HelpServices-Group, a built-in group on member servers.

5. In the Security Options container, configure the following settings:

   ❑ Accounts: Guest account status – Disabled

   ❑ Accounts: Limit local account use of blank passwords to console logon only – Enabled.

❑ Audit: Shut down system immediately if unable to log security events – Disabled.

❑ Devices: Allowed to format and eject removable media – Administrators

❑ Interactive logon: Do not display last user name – Enabled.

❑ Interactive logon: Message text for users attempting to log on – "This system is restricted to authorized users. Individuals attempting unauthorized access will be prosecuted."

❑ Interactive logon: Message title for users attempting to log on "IT IS AN OFFENSE TO CONTINUE WITHOUTH PROPER AUTHORIZATION."

❑ Interactive logon: Number of previous logons to cache (in case domain controller is not available). – 0 logons

❑ Shutdown: Clear virtual memory pagefile – Enabled.

> **NOTE**   Clearing the pagefile does not delete the pagefile, it overwrites the pagefile and is a measure to help remove sensitive information that might reside in the paging file on the hard drive of a computer after the machine has been shut down. National Security Agency Guidelines suggest this option as a method of elevating server security by removing temporary information at shutdown. See the National Security Agency Security Recommendation Guides at *http://acs1.conxion.com/support/*.

❑ System settings: Optional subsystems – <none>

> **NOTE**   If you don't plan on running POSIX or OS2-based programs, supporting those subsystems only opens more pathways through which malicious code can travel.

6. Expand the Member Server Baseline\System Services container.

7. Configure the following settings:

❑ Automatic Updates – Automatic

❑ DHCP Server – Disabled

❑ Distributed File System – Disabled

❑ Event Log – Automatic

❑ File Replication Service – Disabled

❑ Help and Support – Disabled

❑ IIS Admin Service – Disabled

❑ Secondary Logon – Disabled

❑ Task Scheduler – Disabled

> **NOTE**   Remember, you are disabling these services on the Member Server Baseline template, you will still be able to enable the appropriate services on the specialized template that you may make for each sub-organizational unit. The template and policy that is nearest the object will have the highest priority and therefore override the service settings in this step.

Creating and Configuring the Default File Server Security Template

In this section, you will create another security template named Default File Server template. Follow these steps:

1. In the My Security Template Console, create a new template named **Default File Server**.

2. In the Default File Server\System Services container, configure the following settings:

❑ Distributed File System – Disabled

❑ File Replication Service – Disabled

> **NOTE**   You should rename the local administrator account on each file server to a unique name. You cannot do this with templates. Although there is a policy setting titled, "Accounts: Rename Administrator Account", it would provide the same renamed account name on each member of the OU to which it was applied. This does not create a unique name on each server.

3. Close the My Security Template Console. When you close the console, you will be prompted to save the templates that you have created. Be certain to confirm that you want to save your custom templates.

EXERCISE 11-3: USING THE TEMPLATES TO CREATE AND APPLY SECURITY SETTINGS THROUGH GROUP POLICIES

Estimated completion time: 20 minutes

Your manager instructs you to create new group policies based on the existing templates you've built in the previous exercise. You need to enforce a domain-wide security policy and you would like to customize that policy for the member servers on the network.

IMPORTANT If you have two computers, complete the following tasks on Computerxx. If you are working with a partner, you and your lab partner should separately complete the following tasks on your designated computer. Some steps have computer specific instructions.

1. Open the Active Directory Users and Computer console.

2. Right-click the domain and select Properties.

3. Select the Group Policy tab and then click Open to open the Group Policy Management console.

4. In the Group Policy Management console, right-click the domain and select Create And Link A GPO Here.

5. In the New GPO dialog box enter the name **Customized Domain Policy** and click OK.

6. Right-click the new GPO and select Edit.

   The Group Policy Object Editor opens.

7. Expand the Computer Configuration\Windows Settings\Security Settings section.

8. Select the Security Settings node.

9. Click the Action menu and then click Import Policy.

10. In the Import Policy From dialog box, import the Domain Level Security Template created earlier.

11. Close the Group Policy Object Editor.

12. In the Group Policy Management console, move the Customized Domain Policy to the top of the list of linked policies list for the domain.

13. Right-click the Customized Domain Policy and select Enforced.

14. Click OK in the message box asking if you want to change the Enforced setting.

    QUESTION What Windows 2000 GPO option is the Enforced option equivalent to?

15. Use the Group Policy Management console to create a Baseline Member Server Group Policy for the Member Servers OU. Create the new policy by importing the Member Server Baseline template created in Exercise 1-2. Do not set the Enforced setting.

16. Use the Group Policy Management console to create a File Server Group Policy for the File Servers OU. Create the new policy by importing the Default File Server template created in Exercise 1-2. Do not set the Enforced setting.

EXERCISE 11-4: MODELING RESULTANT SET OF POLICY USING THE GROUP POLICY MANAGEMENT CONSOLE

Estimated completion time: 15 minutes

Before you actually start moving production servers into the OU for which you have created security policies, you want to check that the end result is as you planned. You have read that the Group Policy Management console can be used to model the influence of all group policies applied to objects within a domain.

> **IMPORTANT**   If you have two computers, complete the following tasks on Computerxx. If you are working with a partner, you and your lab partner should separately complete the following tasks on your designated computer. Some steps have computer specific instructions.

To perform this modeling:

1. Open Active Directory Users and Computers and select the File Servers OU.

2. Right-click the File Servers OU and select New, Computer.

   The New Object – Computer dialog box opens.

3. Set the Computer name to **RSOP-TEST**. Click Next.

4. Click Next again. Click Finish.

   The RSOP-TEST computer object appears in the File Servers OU.

5. Open the Group Policy Management console.

6. Select the contoso domain object.

7. From the Action menu select Group Policy Modeling Wizard. Click Next.

8. On the Domain Controllers Selection page, click Next.

9. On the User And Computer Selection page (shown below in Figure 11-2), select the Computer option in the Computer Information section. Enter the information for the RSOP-TEST computer.

10. Check the Skip To The Final Page Of This Wizard Without Collecting Additional Data check box. Click Next.

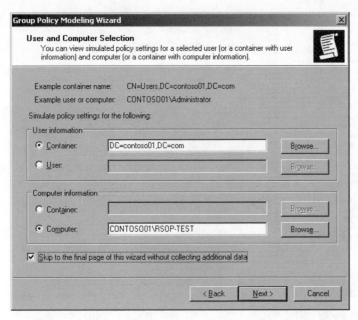

Figure 11-2 Selecting the RSOP-TEST computer in the Group Policy Modeling Wizard.

11. On the Summary Of Selections page, click Next.

   The simulation will run.

12. To view the results, click Finish.

13. Explore the results as shown in Figure 11-3 to determine which settings are configured after the Customized Domain Policy, Baseline Member Server Group Policy, and File Server Group Policy have been applied.

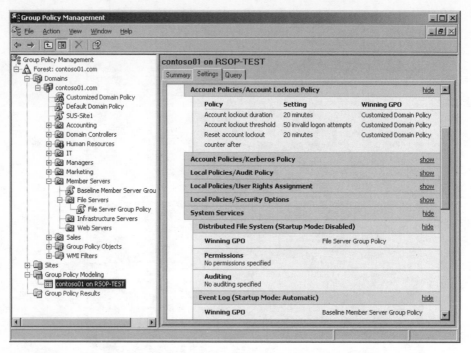

Figure 11-3   Selecting the RSOP-TEST computer in the Group Policy Modeling Wizard.

> **NOTE**   Depending on how you configured the Enforced setting, you may get different results for Group Policy Modeling.

14. Close the Group Policy Management console

REVIEW QUESTIONS

Estimated completion time: 15 minutes

1. In your words, describe what you learned during this lab.

2. What are methods of applying security settings in a step-wise fashion? To which OU do you apply the most restrictive settings? Why?

3. How does inheritance of Group Policy apply to child domains? How does inheritance apply to child OUs?

4. On which tab of Group Policy Modeling results can you determine the effective Local Policies/Security Options?

5. How can you block the Enforced option for Group Policy settings that are configured on parent container?

LAB CHALLENGE 11-1: CREATING MORE TEMPLATES AND POLICIES

Estimated completion time: 25 minutes

You are a network administrator for the Contosoxx.com domain. In order to configure the infrastructure server settings so that they are applicable to DHCP and WINS servers and you must configure Web server attributes as well. In this exercise, you will take the skills you've learned in this lab and extend them to the two remaining un-customized Infrastructure Servers and Web Servers OUs. This will require the creation of two new templates and two new group policies that will separately import the appropriate template settings.

Essentially, to maintain the strictest security and most conservative adjustments, you will modify the system services for each template to enable the proper services to run automatically. The fewer the services that are running, the fewer the ports that are communicating on your server and the more secure your server will be. Therefore, you need to enable the following settings:

1. Infrastructure Server:

   System Services

   - ❑ DHCP Server – Automatic

   - ❑ Windows Internet Name Service Server – Automatic

2. Web Server

   System Services

   - ❑ IIS Admin Service – Automatic

   HTTP SSL – Automatic

   - ❑ The HTTP SSL service enables IIS to perform Secure Sockets Layer (SSL) functions.

   - ❑ World Wide Web Publishing Service – Automatic

   Local Policies\User Rights Assignment

   - ❑ Deny access to the computer from the network – ANONYMOUS LOGON, Built-in Administrator, Support_388945a0, and Guest.

   > **NOTE**   You have chosen not to add the Guests group to "deny access" because the IUSR account used for anonymous access to IIS is by default a member of the Guests group. Removing the Guest group ensures anonymous access to IIS servers.

To complete this challenge, create two new security templates named Default Infrastructure Server and Default Web Server. Create two new GPOs named Infrastructure Server Group Policy and Web Server Group Policy. Create IN01 and WEB01 computer object to test the group policy results. Take a screen shot of the results or create a RSoP report with the Group Policy Management console.

POST-LAB CLEANUP

Estimated completion time: 5 minutes

Remove DHCP and WINS services before proceeding to Lab 12.

1. Open the Add Or Remove Programs control panel and click Add/ Remove Windows Components.

   The Windows Component Wizard opens.

2. In the list of components, select Networking Services and click Details.

   The Networking Services dialog box opens.

3. Clear the check marks next to Dynamic Host Configuration Protocol (DHCP) and Windows Internet Name Service (WINS) and then click OK.

4. Click Next to remove the components. You might be asked to insert your Windows Server 2003 CD.

5. When the wizard completes, click Finish.

TROUBLESHOOTING SERVER SECURITY AND DNS

Troubleshooting Lab C is a practical application of the knowledge you have acquired from Labs 9 through 11. Your instructor or lab assistant has changed you computer configuration, causing it to "break." Your task in this lab will be to apply your acquired skills to troubleshoot and resolve the break. A scenario will be presented which will lay out the parameters of the break and the conditions that must be met for the scenario to be resolved. This troubleshooting lab has two break scenarios. The first break scenario involves server security and the second break scenario involves DNS.

> **NOTE** **Do not proceed with this lab until you receive guidance from your instructor.** The break scenario that you will be performing will depend on which computer you are using. The first computer will be Computerxx and the second computer will be Computeryy. Computerxx typically has an odd-numbered name, such as Computer01 and Computer03. Computeryy typically has an even numbered name, such as Computer02 and Computer04 . If you are unsure of your computers name, run a command prompt and issue the **hostname** command. If you are using Computerxx, you will perform Break Scenario 1. If you are using Computeryy, you will perform Break Scenario 2. Your instructor or lab assistant may also have special instructions. Consult with your instructor before proceeding.

Break Scenario 1

> **IMPORTANT** Perform this break scenario on Computerxx.

Contoso, Ltd. is a large accounting firm with offices in twenty cities. The company network contains five member servers running Windows Server 2003, Standard Edition, 200 client computers running Windows XP Professional, and three domain controllers running Windows Server 2003, Enterprise Edition. All computers are configured in a single Active Directory site.

One of the Windows Server 2003 systems is running IIS and hosts the company's public Web site and FTP site. A recent update of security policies has occurred. Unfortunately, this update has meant that the company's Web site and FTP site are no longer available. Determine why the company's web site and FTP site are no longer available and resolve this issue.

As you resolve the problem, fill out the worksheet in the TroubleshootingLabC folder and include the following information:

- Description of the problem.

- A list of all steps taken to diagnose the problem, even the ones that did not work.

- Description of the exact issue and solution.

- A list of the tools and resources you used to help solve this problem.

Break Scenario 2

Perform this break scenario on Computeryy.

> **NOTE** Ensure that you log on to Computeryy and complete this exercise using the account Administrator@contosoxx.com account rather than the Administrator@contosoyy.contosoxx.com account. Ensure also that the DNS servers for Computerxx and Computeryy appear in the DNS console.

Contoso, Ltd's DNS servers host zones not only for Contoso Ltd, but also for subsidiary companies Proseware and Litware, Inc. These DNS zones are hosted on two servers that function as domain controllers, one located in the Contoso, Ltd root domain and another located in a child domain.

Several name resolution irregularities have arisen on both the DNS server located in the root domain and on the server located in the child domain. Your manager has asked you to investigate the following:

- Why clients cannot use the DNS server on Computeryy to resolve queries for the prosewarexx.com zone. For example, the host, challenge.prosewarexx.com cannot be resolved on clients that use Computeryy as a DNS server.

- Why Computeryy cannot process updates to the Contosoxx.com zone.

- Why clients cannot use the DNS server on Computer*xx* to resolve queries for the litwareincyy.com zone, but can resolve queries for the sub.litwareincyy.com zone. For example, the host challenge.litwareincyy.com cannot be resolved, but the host record challenge.sub.litwareincyy.com can be resolved on clients that use Computer*xx* as a DNS server.

As you resolve the problem, fill out the worksheet in the TroubleshootingLabC folder and include the following information:

- Description of the problem.

- A list of all steps taken to diagnose the problem, even the ones that did not work.

- Description of the exact issue and solution.

- A list of the tools and resources you used to help solve this problem.

LAB 12
DATA BACKUP AND RECOVERY

Upon completion of this chapter, you will be able to:

- Exercise 12-1: Performing Data Backup

- Exercise 12-2: Performing Data Restoration

- Exercise 12-3: Scheduling Backup Jobs

- Exercise 12-4: Using Shadow Copies of Shared Folders

- Lab Review Questions

- Lab Challenge 12-1: Designing a Backup Strategy

- Post-Lab Cleanup

SCENARIO

You are a domain administrator for Contoso, Ltd.. Contoso has a large multi-domain Active Directory network with contoso*xx*.com as its root domain. You are responsible for the design and implementation of a backup strategy suitable for meeting the goals of the company's disaster-recovery policies. Specific duties include the following:

- Designing a disaster-recovery strategy for specified user data

- Implementing the disaster-recovery strategy for specified user data

- Perform a normal backup

- Perform a differential backup

- Perform an incremental backup

- Schedule a backup job

- Run a backup job from the command line

- Recover a file from Shadow Copies of Shared Folders

After completing this lab, you will be able to:

- Perform different types of backups
- Restore backups
- Schedule backup jobs
- Use shadow copies for shared folders

Estimated lesson time: 130 minutes

BEFORE YOU BEGIN

To successfully complete this lab, you will need the following:

- A computer with Windows Server 2003 installed and configured as a domain controller. (See Lab Exercises 2-1 and 2-2.)

- The computer should have its own domain, which will either be contoso*xx*.com or contoso*yy*.contoso*xx*.com.

> **NOTE**   This lab is written to be performed on two computers. If each student has only a single computer, students can work as partners and share computers when needed. The first computer will be Computerxx and the second computer will be Computeryy. Computerxx typically has an odd-numbered name, such as Computer01 and Computer03. Computeryy typically has an even numbered name, such as Computer02 and Computer04 . If you are unsure of your computers name, run a command prompt and issue the **hostname** command.

EXERCISE 12-1: PERFORMING BACKUPS

Estimated completion time: 30 minutes

In this exercise, you will create several different types of backup jobs, identifying the unique characteristics of each.

> **IMPORTANT**   If you have two computers, complete the following tasks on Computerxx. If you are working with a partner, you and your lab partner should separately complete the following tasks on your designated computer.

Normal Backup

In this portion of the exercise, you will create a file and perform a normal backup.

1. Log on to the computer as **Administrator**. The password is **P@ssw0rd**. For Computer*xx*, select the contoso*xx* domain. For Computer*yy*, select the contoso*yy* domain.

2. Create a folder named **C:\Lab 12 Backups**. Create a second folder named **C:\Lab 12 Data**.

> **NOTE**   This folder will contain all of the data used in this lab. In a production environment, data backups are performed to an external device such as a tape drive. If you have a tape drive available, you may use it for these exercises by substituting the tape drive for any backup target locations specified.

3. Using Notepad, create a new file containing one line of text. Save the file as "**C:\Lab 12 Data\BackupData.txt**" (include the quotes).

4. Open a command prompt, change to the C:\Lab 12 Data\ directory, and issue the **attrib** command. Note the attributes listed for the BackupData.txt file.

> **QUESTION**   What do the attributes listed next to the BackupData.txt file mean? If unsure, use the **attrib /?** command or the Help and Support Center.

5. Open the Backup Utility by running Ntbackup from the Run menu or by selecting Backup from the All Programs\Accessories\System Tools group on the Start menu.

6. Clear the Always Start in In Wizard Mode check box.

7. Click the Advanced Mode hyperlink on the welcome page.

   The Backup Utility opens in advanced mode.

8. Select the Backup tab.

9. Expand My Computer and expand the C:\ drive.

10. Add a check mark next to the Lab 12 Data folder as shown in Figure 12-1.

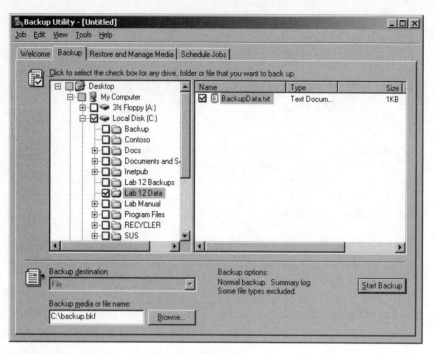

Figure 12-1   Selections in the Backup Utility.

11. On the Job menu, choose Save Selections.

The Save As dialog box opens.

12. Save the selections as Lab 12 Data.bks in the default folder.

13. On the Backup tab, in the Backup Media Or Filename box, type:
C:\Lab 12 Backups\backup-normal.bkf.

14. Click Start Backup.

The Backup Job Information dialog box opens.

15. Click Advanced.

The Advanced Backup Options dialog box opens.

16. Confirm that Normal is selected in the Backup Type drop-down box, and then click OK.

17. Select Replace The Data On The Media With This Backup and click Start Backup.

The Backup Progress dialog box opens showing the progress.

18. Observe the Backup Progress dialog box. When the backup is complete, click Report.

19. Examine the report. No errors should be reported.

20. Close the report and close the Backup Progress dialog box.

> **QUESTION** After you finish the backup, is the archive attribute for BackupData.txt still set? Why or why not?

Differential Backup

In this portion of the exercise, you will perform a differential backup.

1. Open the file C:\Lab 12 Data\BackupData.txt, add a line of text, and save the file.

> **QUESTION** What will happen to the archive attribute after step 1?

2. In the Backup Utility, select the Backup tab.

3. On the Job menu, choose Load Selections.

4. In the Open dialog box, select Lab 12 Data.bks. Click Open.

5. On the Backup tab, in the Backup Media Or Filename box, type: **C:\Lab 12 Backups\backup-differential.bkf**.

6. Click Start Backup and then click Advanced.

7. Select Differential in the Backup Type drop-down box and then click OK.

8. Select Replace The Data On The Media With This Backup and click Start Backup.

9. Observe the Backup Progress dialog box. When the backup is complete, click Report.

10. Examine the report. No errors should be reported.

11. Close the report and close the Backup Progress dialog box.

> **QUESTION** What is different about the archive attribute on the backed up file now as compared to when you performed a normal backup?

Incremental Backup

In this portion of the exercise, you will perform an incremental backup.

1. Open the file C:\Lab 12 Data\BackupData.txt, add a line of text, and save the file.

2. In the Backup Utility, select the Backup tab.

3. On the Job menu, choose Load Selections.

4. In the Open dialog box, select Lab 12 Data.bks. Click Open.

5. On the Backup tab, in the Backup Media Or Filename box, type:
    C:\Lab 12 Data\backup-incremental.bkf.

6. Click Start Backup and then click Advanced.

7. Select Incremental in the Backup Type drop-down box and then click
    OK.

8. Select Replace The Data On The Media With This Backup and click
    Start Backup.

9. Observe the Backup Progress dialog box. When the backup is
    complete, click Report.

10. Examine the report. No errors should be reported.

11. Close the report and close the Backup Progress dialog box.

> **QUESTION**   What happens to the archive attribute when you perform an
> incremental backup?

EXERCISE 12-2: PERFORMING DATA RESTORATION

Estimated completion time: 20 minutes

In this exercise, you will perform a restoration for each of the backup files you
created in the previous exercise.

> **IMPORTANT**   If you have two computers, complete the following tasks
> on Computerxx. If you are working with a partner, you and your lab partner
> should separately complete the following tasks on your designated
> computer.

Restoring the Normal Backup

In this portion of the exercise, you will restore the BackupData.txt using the
backup-normal.bkf file.

1. In the Backup Utility, click the Restore And Manage Media tab.

2. Click the plus sign to expand the File node.

3. Click the plus sign to expand Backup-normal.bkf.

4. Click the check box to select C:.

5. Select the C: node.

6. Expand the C: node. You will notice that your selection of the C: folder has selected its child folders and files as shown in Figure 12-2.

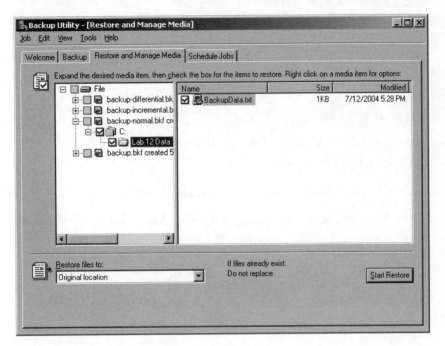

Figure 12-2 Items to restore.

7. In the Restore Files To drop-down box, select Alternate Location.

8. In the Alternate Location box, type **C:\Lab 12 Backups\TestRestore**.

9. Click Start Restore.

10. In the Confirm Restore dialog box, click OK.

11. Observe the Restore Progress dialog box. If the Check Backup File Location dialog box appears, click OK.

12. Close the Restore Progress dialog box.

> **QUESTION** Which version of the BackupData.txt file do you expect to be restored?

13. Examine the BackupData.txt file restored in C:\Lab 12 Backups\TestRestore\Lab 12 Data.

Restoring the Differential Backup

In this portion of the exercise, you will restore the BackupData.txt file using the backup-differential.bkf file.

1. In the Backup Utility, click the Restore And Manage Media tab.

2. Click the plus sign to expand the File node.

3. Click the plus sign to expand Backup-differential.bkf.

4. Click the check box to select C:.

5. Select the C: node.

6. Expand the C: node. You will notice that your selection of the C: folder has selected its child folders and files.

7. In the Restore Files To drop-down box, select Alternate Location.

8. In the Alternate Location field, type **C:\Lab 12 Backups\TestRestore**.

9. Click Start Restore.

10. In the Confirm Restore dialog box, click OK.

11. Observe the Restore Progress dialog box. If the Check Backup File Location dialog box appears, click OK.

12. Close the Restore Progress dialog box.

> **QUESTION**   Which version of the BackupData.txt file do you expect to be restored? Why?

ANSWER

> No version was restored. Because a previous file existed, that file was not replaced.

13. Examine the BackupData.txt file restored in C:\Lab 12 Backups\TestRestore\Lab 12 Data.

14. In the Backup Utility, click the Tools menu and then click Options.

    The Options dialog box opens.

15. Click the Restore tab.

16. Select Always Replace The File On My Computer.

17. Click OK.

18. Repeat Steps 3 through 13 and the second version of the file, with two lines of text, should be restored.

Restoring the Incremental Backup

In this portion of the exercise, you will restore the BackupData.txt file using the backup-incremental.bkf file.

1. In the Backup Utility, click the Restore And Manage Media tab.

2. Click the plus sign to expand the File node.

3. Click the plus sign to expand Backup-incremental.bkf.

4. Click the check box to select C:.

5. Select the C: node.

6. Expand the C: node. You will notice that your selection of the C: folder has selected its child folders and files.

7. In the Restore Files To drop-down box, select Alternate Location.

8. In the Alternate Location field, type **C:\Lab 12 Backups \TestRestor**e.

9. Click Start Restore.

10. In the Confirm Restore dialog box, click OK.

11. Observe the Restore Progress dialog box. If the Check Backup File Location dialog box appears, click OK.

12. Close the Restore Progress dialog box.

> **QUESTION** Which version of the BackupData.txt file do you expect to be restored?

13. Examine the BackupData.txt file restored in C:\Lab 12 Back-ups\TestRestore\Lab 12 Data.

> **QUESTION** Why, if you have multiple incremental backup sets, do you need to restore them in the order in which the backups were made?

EXERCISE 12-3: SCHEDULING BACKUP JOBS

Estimated completion time: 15 minutes

In this exercise, you will schedule a backup job from Exercise 12-1 to begin daily at midnight.

IMPORTANT   If you have two computers, complete the following tasks on Computerxx. If you are working with a partner, you and your lab partner should separately complete the following tasks on your designated computer.

Scheduling a Backup Job

1. In the Backup Utility, select the Backup tab.

2. On the Job menu, choose Load Selections. Select Lab 12 Data.bks, and choose Open.

3. In the Backup Media Or File Name box, type **C:\Lab 12 Back-ups\backup-scheduled.bkf**.

4. Click Start Backup and then click Schedule.

   NOTE   There are several different methods to schedule a backup job. Many administrators find it easiest to create the backup job and then schedule the job directly in the Backup Utility.

5. In the Set Account Information dialog box, type your Administrator password (**P@ssw0rd**) in each text box to be used for the scheduled backup job, and click OK.

   The Scheduled Job Options dialog box opens.

6. Enter **Lab 12 Scheduled Backup** in the Job Name textbox, then click Properties.

   The Schedule Job dialog box opens.

7. In the Schedule Task dropdown box, select Daily, and select 12:00 AM as the Start Time as shown in Figure 12-3.

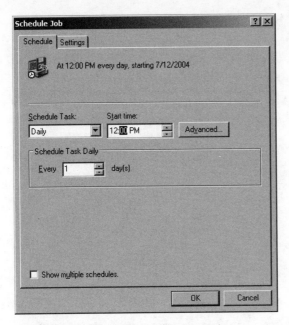

Figure 12-3   Scheduling a backup job.

8. Click OK to close the Schedule Job properties dialog box. If the Set Account Information dialog box appears again, type your Administrator password in each text box and click OK.

9. Click OK to close the Scheduled Job Options properties dialog box.

10. Click the Welcome tab, then click the Schedule Jobs tab to refresh the display. You should see the scheduled job icons displayed on each day of the System Event calendar as shown in Figure 12-4.

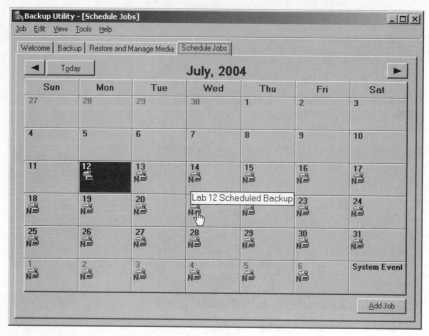

Figure 12-4   Schedule job calendar.

NOTE   You can also view and modify scheduled backup jobs from the Scheduled Tasks utility in Control Panel.

Running a Backup Job from the Command Prompt Window

In this portion of the exercise, you will use the scheduled job to help you create a functionally identical command line. You will then analyze the command line to identify the function of the switches used.

1. In the Schedule Jobs calendar, click the icon, representing the Lab 12 Scheduled Backup job.

2. In the Scheduled Job Options dialog box, click Properties.

3. Select the command in the Run box, and press Ctrl+C to copy it.

4. Click Cancel to close the Schedule Job dialog box and click Cancel to close Schedule Job Options dialog box.

5. Close the Backup Utility.

6. Open a Command Prompt window.

7. Right-click in the Command Prompt window and choose Paste from the context menu. The Ntbackup command with all of its switches is pasted into the Command Prompt window.

8. Press Enter. The Backup Utility opens and the Lab 12 Scheduled Backup job is executed.

9. Open a new file in Notepad. Paste the text of the backup command into the document.

> **QUESTION** Which switch indicates the type of backup job being performed? (if unsure, issue the ntbackup /? command)

> **QUESTION** What are some key settings you might change in the command line if using it repeatedly in a batch file?

EXERCISE 12-4: USING SHADOW COPIES OF SHARED FOLDERS

Estimated completion time: 20 minutes

In this exercise, you will enable and configure options for Shadow Copies of Shared Folders for the C:\ drive.

If you have two computers, complete the following tasks on Computerxx. If you are working with a partner, you and your lab partner should separately complete the following tasks on your designated computer.

Enable Shadow Copies of Shared Folders

In this portion of the exercise, you will share the Lab 12 Data folder and enable Shadow Copies of Shared Folders on the C:\ drive.

1. Using Windows Explorer, share the C:\Lab 12 Data folder as Lab 12 Data. Set share permissions so that the Everyone group is allowed Full Control.

2. Right-click the C:\ drive icon and choose Properties.

3. Click the Shadow Copies tab and click Enable to enable Shadow Copies of Shared Folders on the C:\ drive. In the message box that appears, click Yes.

4. Click the Create Now button to create the Shadow Copies of Share Foldersof the volume. The Shadow Copies tab is shown in Figure 12-5.

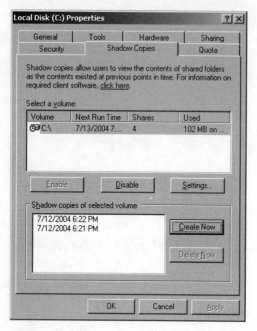

Figure 12-5   The Shadow Copies tab of the Local Disk properties.

Recover a file using Shadow Copies of Shared Folders

In this portion of the exercise, you will delete a file and recover it from the Shadow Copies of Shared Folders.

1. Using Windows Explorer, open the C:\Lab 12 Data folder and delete the BackupData.txt file.

2. Close Windows Explorer.

3. Open the share through UNC by clicking Start, choosing Run and entering \\localhost

   > **NOTE**   You must connect to Shadow Copies of Shared Folders through UNC in order to see previous versions.

4. To recover the deleted BackupData.txt file, right-click the Lab 12 Data folder and choose Properties.

5. Select the Previous Versions tab as shown in Figure 12-6.

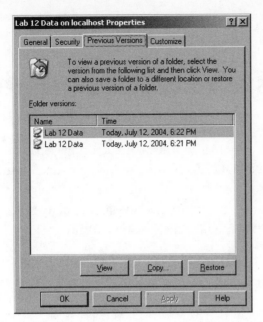

Figure 12-6   The Previous Versions tab of the share's properties.

6. Select the the most recent Lab 12 Data folder and click View.

> **QUESTION**   *What is the full name of the window that opens, as shown in the window's title bar?*

7. Right-click the BackupData.txt file and choose Copy.

8. Using Windows Explorer, open the current Lab 12 Data folder.

9. Paste the BackupData.txt file into the folder.

REVIEW QUESTIONS

Estimated completion time: 15 minutes

1. What are the fundamental differences among normal, differential, and incremental backups?

2. What are some key advantages to using a true backup versus using a Shadow Copies of Shared Folders?

3. What are some key advantages to using Shadow Copies of Shared Folders versus a true backup?

4. If you take a normal backup on Monday at 6:00 P.M. and and an incremental backup on Tuesday, Wednesday, and Thursday at 7:00 P.M., in what order should you perform a restore of all data if a failure occurs on Thursday at 10:00 P.M.? (assume that the Thursday backup has finished at that time).

LAB CHALLENGE 12-1: DESIGNING A BACKUP STRATEGY

Estimated completion time: 25 minutes

You are asked to configure a backup strategy for the Manufacturing Department's data. The backup should occur automatically during the early-morning hours because there are users working shifts from 4:00 A.Mm to 12:00 midnight, Monday through Friday. Files in the folder change frequently: about half the files change once a week; the other half of the files change almost daily.

- **Your objectives, in order of priority, are:**   All data from the previous day's activity should be backed up and available for restoration.

- Downtime should be minimized: restorations should be optimized to perform as quickly as possible.

- **The constraints to your backup strategy are:**   A complete normal backup of the data takes six hours.

Describe, in detail, your backup strategy.

POST-LAB CLEANUP

Estimated completion time: 5 minutes

To remove the scheduled backups created in this lab and disable Shadow Copies for Shared Folders, perform these steps:

1. Click Start, All Programs, Accessories, System Tools, and then Scheduled Tasks.

2. Delete the scheduled backup tasks created in this lab (Lab 12 Scheduled Backup, Nightly D Backups, and Sunday F Backups).

3. Open the Properties dialog box for the C:\ drive.

4. On the Shadow Copies tab, click Disable and then click Yes to confirm.

LAB 13
RECOVERING FROM SYSTEM FAILURE

Upon completion of this chapter, you will be able to:

■ Exercise 13-1: Backing up Active Directory

■ Exercise 13-2: Restoring Active Directory

■ Exercise 13-3: Performing an Authoritative Restore

■ Exercise 13-4: Using the Recovery Console

■ Lab Review Questions

■ Lab Challenge 13-1: Creating an Automated System Recovery Backup Set

SCENARIO

You are a domain administrator for Contoso, Ltd. Contoso, Ltd. has a large multi-domain Active Directory network with contoso.com as its root domain. You are responsible for the design and implementation of a backup strategy suitable for meeting the goals of the company's disaster recovery policies. When you follow the objectives in this lab, you will:

■ Design a disaster recovery strategy for domain controllers

■ Implement the disaster recovery strategy for domain controllers

■ Perform a backup of Active Directory

■ Perform a restore of Active Directory

■ Perform an authoritative restore

■ Install and use the Recovery Console

■ Create an Automated System Recovery backup set

BEFORE YOU BEGIN

To successfully complete this lab, you will need the following:

- A computer with Windows Server 2003 installed and configured as a domain controller. (See Lab Exercises 2-1 and 2-2.)

- The computer should have its own domain, which will either be contosoxx.com or contosoyy.contosoxx.com.

> **NOTE** This lab is written to be performed on two computers. If each student has only a single computer, students can work as partners and share computers when needed. The first computer will be Computerxx and the second computer will be Computeryy. Computerxx typically has an odd-numbered name, such as Computer01 and Computer03. Computeryy typically has an even numbered name, such as Computer02 and Computer04 . If you are unsure of your computers name, run a command prompt and issue the **hostname** command.

After completing this lab, you will be able to:

- Back up Active Directory
- Restore Active Directory
- Perform an authoritative restore
- Use the recovery console

Estimated lesson time: 125 minutes

EXERCISE 13-1: BACKING UP ACTIVE DIRECTORY

Estimated Completion Time: 15 minutes

In this exercise, you will back up the System State, which contains all of the components of Active Directory.

> **IMPORTANT** If you have two computers, complete the following tasks on Computerxx. If you are working with a partner, you and your lab partner should separately complete the following tasks on your designated computer.

1. Log on to the computer as **Administrator**. The password is **P@ssw0rd**. For Computerxx, select the contosoxx domain. For Computeryy, select the contosoyy domain.

2. Create a folder on the C:\ drive named Lab 13 Backups.

3. Start the Backup Utility.

4. Click the Backup tab, and select the check box next to System State.

5. Select the System State label so that you can see the components of the System State listed in the right pane, as shown in Figure 13-1.

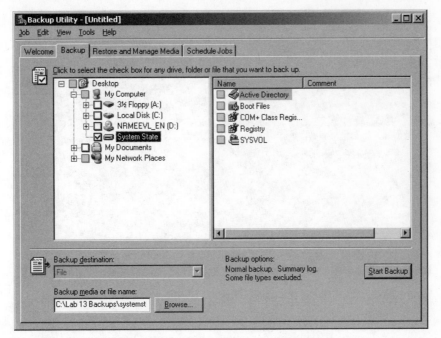

Figure 13-1   System State components ready for backup.

6. In the Backup Media Or File Name box, type the backup file name **C:\Lab 13 Backups\SystemState.bkf**.

7. Start the backup. Backup will take a few minutes to complete.

8. When the backup is complete, examine the file size of the System State backup file.

QUESTION   How big is the file?

EXERCISE 13-2: RESTORING ACTIVE DIRECTORY

Estimated completion time: 20 minutes

In this exercise, you will restore Active Directory (System State) that you backed up during the previous exercise.

IMPORTANT   If you have two computers, complete the following tasks on Computerxx. If you are working with a partner, you and your lab partner should separately complete the following tasks on your designated computer.

1. Restart the computer.

2. As the computer boots, press F8 to display the Windows Advanced Options Menu as shown in Figure 13-2.

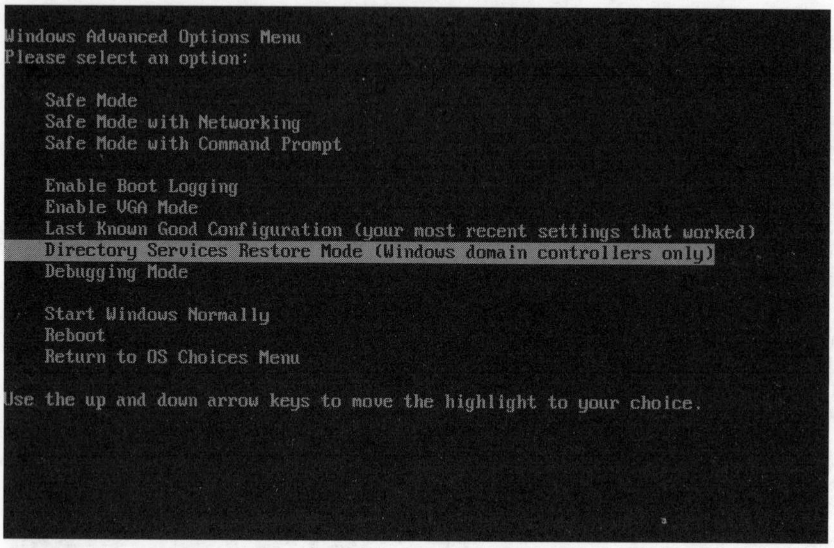

```
Windows Advanced Options Menu
Please select an option:

    Safe Mode
    Safe Mode with Networking
    Safe Mode with Command Prompt

    Enable Boot Logging
    Enable VGA Mode
    Last Known Good Configuration (your most recent settings that worked)
    Directory Services Restore Mode (Windows domain controllers only)
    Debugging Mode

    Start Windows Normally
    Reboot
    Return to OS Choices Menu

Use the up and down arrow keys to move the highlight to your choice.
```

Figure 13-2 Windows Advanced Options Menu

3. Select Directory Services Restore Mode (Windows Domain Controllers Only) and press ENTER. This ensures that Active Directory on this domain controller is offline.

4. If you are asked to select the operating system to start, select Windows Server 2003, Enterprise and press ENTER.

5. Log on as Administrator. The password is the Directory Services Restore Mode Administrator password specified in Lab 2, **P@ssw0rd**.

> **NOTE** When you restart the computer in Directory Services Restore Mode, you must log on as Administrator using the Directory Services Restore Mode Administrator password, *not* the Administrator password for the contoso domain. The Directory Services Restore Mode Administrator password was supplied when the computer was promoted to the role of a domain controller in Lab 2. To simplify things, the Directory Services Restore Mode Administrator password was set to the same password as the Administrator password for the domain, though in a real life situation this might not be the case.

6. In the Desktop message box that warns you that Windows is running in safe mode, click OK.

7. Start the Backup Utility.

8. On the Welcome tab, click the Restore Wizard (Advanced) button.

The Restore Wizard opens.

9. On the What To Restore page, select the System State data for C:\Lab 13 Backups\SystemState.bkf as shown in Figure 13-3.

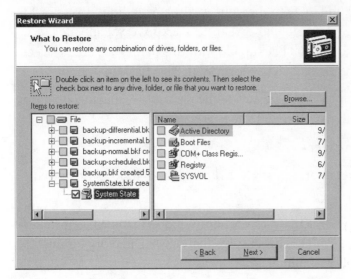

Figure 13-3   Preparing to restore the System State data.

10. Click Next and then click Finish.

11. In the Warning message box that warns you that restoring System State will always overwrite current System State, click OK to start the restore process.

12. When prompted to restart the computer, click Yes.

EXERCISE 13-3: PERFORMING AN AUTHORITATIVE RESTORE

Estimated completion time: 30 minutes

In this exercise, you will create an Organizational Unit, back up the System State, delete the Organizational Unit, then restore the Organizational Unit authoritatively.

> **IMPORTANT**   If you have two computers, complete the following tasks on Computerxx. If you are working with a partner, you and your lab partner should separately complete the following tasks on your designated computer.

1. Log on to the computer as Administrator.

2. Using Active Directory Users and Computers, create a root-level Organizational Unit named Phrenology.

3. Create two new users in the Phrenology OU named Orin and Sue.

4. Using the Backup Utility in the same way that you did in Exercise 13-1, backup the System State to C:\Lab 13 Backups\SystemState.bkf. Since you already have a backup file with this name, be sure to select the Replace The Data On The Media With This Backup option.

5. After the backup is complete, delete the Phrenology Organizational Unit, along with the Orin and Sue user objects.

6. Restart the computer.

7. As the computer boots, press F8 to display the Windows Advanced Options Menu.

8. Select Directory Services Restore Mode (Windows Domain Controllers Only) and press ENTER. This ensures that Active Directory on this domain controller is offline.

9. If you are asked to select the operating system to start, select Windows Server 2003, Enterprise and press ENTER.

10. Log on as Administrator using the Directory Services Restore Mode Administrator password.

11. In the Desktop message box that warns you that Windows is running in safe mode, click OK.

12. Start the Backup Utility.

13. On the Welcome tab, click The Restore Wizard (Advanced) button.

   The Restore Wizard opens.

14. On the What To Restore page, select the System State data for C:\Lab 13 Backups\SystemState.bkf.

15. Click Next and then click Finish.

16. In the Warning message box that warns you that restoring System State will always overwrite current System State, click OK to start the restore process.

17. When prompted to restart the computer, click No.

18. Open a command prompt window.

19. At the command line, type **ntdsutil** and press ENTER.

20. At the Ntdsutil prompt, type **authoritative restore** and press ENTER.

21. At the Ntdsutil\authoritative restore prompt, type **?** and press ENTER to see help information for Restore commands.

22. If you are using Computerxx, at the Ntdsutil\authoritative restore prompt, type **restore subtree OU=Phrenology,DC=Contosoxx,DC=Com** and press ENTER. If you are using Computeryy, at the Ntdsutil\authoritative restore prompt, type **restore subtree OU=Phrenology,DC=Contosoyy,DC=Contosoxx,DC=Com** and press ENTER.

23. In the Authoritative Restore Confirmation Dialog box, click Yes.

When authoritative restore completes, the number of records successfully updated is listed.

> **QUESTION**   How many records does the authoritative restore update?

24. Type **quit** and press ENTER. Type **quit** and press ENTER again to exit the Ntdsutil utility. Then close the Command Prompt window.

25. Restart the computer.

26. Log on as Administrator.

27. Open Active Directory Users and Computers and verify that the Phrenology OU, Orin user, and Sue user are restored.

> **QUESTION**   In this exercise, you restore System State and then use Ntdsutil to perform an authoritative restore of the Phrenology subtree. A backup of System State was created before the Phrenology OU was deleted, so why is it necessary to use Ntdsutil?

EXERCISE 13-4: USING THE RECOVERY CONSOLE

Estimated completion time: 20 minutes

A computer that has the Recovery Console installed does not complete the boot process. You suspect the problem is related to the Messenger service. However, since you can't start the computer to disable the service, you decide to use the Recovery Console.

> **IMPORTANT**   If you have two computers, complete the following tasks on Computerxx. If you are working with a partner, you and your lab partner should separately complete the following tasks on your designated computer.

Installing the Recovery Console

In this portion of the exercise, you will install the Recovery Console.

1. Log on to the computer as Administrator.

2. Insert the Windows Server 2003 CD-ROM.

3. Open a Command Prompt window and enter the following command:
   cd-drive:**\i386\winnt32 /cmdcons**

4. When asked if you want to install the Recovery Console, click Yes.

5. Follow any prompts to install the Recovery Console. If the installation attempts to download updated files from the Internet, skip the process of getting updated files and let the installer use the local installation files.

> **NOTE** The Recovery Console installation will install the 8 MB console in a hidden folder named Cmdcons, and it will modify the boot.ini file to provide the Recovery Console as a startup option during the boot process.

Using the Recovery Console

In this portion of the exercise, you will configure a service using the Recovery Console.

1. To simulate a service in need of troubleshooting, open the Services console from Administrative Tools.

2. Locate the Messenger service. Double-click the service, choose Automatic as the Startup Type, and click OK.

3. Restart the computer.

4. When the computer presents the startup boot menu, as shown in Figure 13-4, select Microsoft Windows Recovery Console and press ENTER.

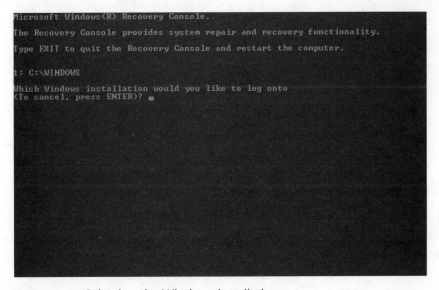

```
Please select the operating system to start:


    Windows Server 2003, Enterprise
    Microsoft Windows Recovery Console

Use the up and down arrow keys to move the highlight to your choice.
Press ENTER to choose.




For troubleshooting and advanced startup options for Windows, press F8.
```

Figure 13-4   Starting the Recovery Console.

5. When prompted to select a Windows installation, as shown in Figure 13-5, type **1** and press ENTER.

```
Microsoft Windows(R) Recovery Console.

The Recovery Console provides system repair and recovery functionality.

Type EXIT to quit the Recovery Console and restart the computer.

1: C:\WINDOWS

Which Windows installation would you like to log onto
<To cancel, press ENTER>? ▪
```

Figure 13-5   Selecting the Windows installation.

6. Type the password for the Administrator account and press ENTER.

7. When the Recovery Console prompt appears (by default, C:\Windows>), type **help** and press ENTER to display a list of commands. Press the spacebar to page through the list.

8. Type **listsvc** and press ENTER to display a list of services and drivers. Press the spacebar to page through the list.

> **NOTE**   Note that the short name of many services is not the same as the long name. However, the short name of the Messenger service is also Messenger. Confirm that its startup is set to Auto (Automatic).

9. Type **disable messenger** and press ENTER to disable the service. The output of the command indicates that the start_type the service has been set to SERVICE_DISABLED.

10. To quit the Recovery Console, type **exit** and press ENTER. The computer is restarted.

11. After the computer restarts, verify that Messenger service is set to Disabled.

REVIEW QUESTIONS

Estimated completion time: 10 minutes

1. What are some key practices that the Recovery Console allows you to perform?

2. What is the primary difference between restoring Active Directory (System State) normally vs. authoritatively?

3. How do you enable a disabled service using the Recovery Console?

4. What command would you issue from the Ntdsutil utility's authoritative restore prompt to recover a child OU of the Accountants OU named Managers in the tailspintoys.com domain?

LAB CHALLENGE 13-1: CREATING AN AUTOMATED SYSTEM RECOVERY BACKUP SET

Estimated completion time: 30 minutes

Unlike Windows NT 4.0 and Windows 2000, Windows Server 2003 does not use emergency repair disks. Replacing this is a new technology called Automated System Recovery (ASR). Your boss has asked you to prepare an ASR backup set. Save this backup as C:\Lab 13 Backups\Asr-set.bkf. When creating an ASR backup, you will need a floppy disk to store some ASR settings.

> **NOTE**   ASR saves the entire contents of your C:\ drive. The resulting ASR backup file will be about 2 GB in size and can take about 20-30 minutes to create. To save time and space, you might choose to just start the process and then cancel the actual ASR backup file creation.